f u se

patrick jones

born tredegar 1965.

educated oakdale, cross keys, swansea.

writer of everything must go (uk tour march 2000), the guerilla tapestry (performed at opening of welsh assembly voices of a nation concert summer 1999), poem for pictures of the gone world (film for bbc wales 1999), unprotected sex (cardiff october 1999).

has survived 30 jobs and four years travelling around the usa.

lives for his children.

PARTHIAN BOOKS

f u se

patrick jones

selected plays
and poetry

Parthian Books
53 Colum Road
Cardiff
CF10 3EF

www.parthianbooks.co.uk

First published in 2001.
All rights reserved.
© Patrick Jones
ISBN 1-902638-15-8

Typeset in Galliard by NW.

Printed and bound by Colourbooks, Dublin.

Published with financial support from the Arts Council
of Wales.

With support from the Parthian Collective.

Cover design by Matt Jon.
Photography by Rhian Ap Gruffydd

A CIP catalogue record for this book is available from
the British Library.

this book is dedicated to:
evan jones ethan jones rebekah bishop victoria bishop
allen jones irene jones
nicholas jones
jane newman
james bradfield sean moore richey edwards

special thanks to:
phil clark kate strudwick margaret rooney & everyone at
blackwood miner's institute
rhian ap gruffydd and lewis davies
and to everyone who has ever supported my work.

f u se

publications:

the guerilla tapestry 1995

the protest of discipline (with david garner) 1996

mute communion 1997

the words are coming
by nicky wire

Back in 1990 we were playing Salisbury arts centre - supporting
the Levellers - as always, in those days, we lasted about 15
minutes, alienating 1000 people and being bottled off. Travelling
back in a cold transit van my brother Patrick, who had come
along for moral support, began reciting - or better, ranting - a
poem. Suddenly everything made sense - alienation felt
comforting - the poem was 'the eloquence in the screaming'
which still inspires me - the moment crystallised - froze and
stayed with me ever since - Patrick had become a poet - we
weren't alone - he had realised himself - our voices had become
one.

This collection traces the development and metamorphosis from
that night - through years of struggle - self financed books -
fatherhood - silence and 30 jobs where the only vocation was
writing. These poems are bitter but beautiful - angry yet tender -
loving though full of hatred. They are the writer bearing witness
to all this........... life. From the yearning societal scream of *the
guerilla tapestry* to the more personal tragedy of modern
masculinity in *father's day 2000*, these poems are unafraid to
connect and force the reader to question one's own being.

To declare yourself a poet today is the maddest of ideas - open to
ridicule - financially perilous - the search for an audience when so
much writing is based on hype, style, celebrity or what writing

course you attended - the mere fact that this collection exists is a
triumph in itself.

It lives - it breathes - it questions - it still screams - it defies
cynicism, embraces truth and kisses reality. From the tiniest
epiphany to the most massive gesture, these words should be
studied and enjoyed by everyone.

As Camus said, 'the struggle itself is enough to fill a human
heart'- open your arteries - the words are coming -

```
nicky wire
    2001
```

new & selected poetry

"it does not matter to be the stone,
the dark stone,
the pure stone which the river bears away"

pablo neruda

"i hear that they call life our only refuge"

paul celan

contents

this terrible honesty

i don't think i'll ever understand this
these   the
long hours of sorrow stabbed friendship i feel here
so close your eyes/ fold your hands/ lie calm
let this darkness shroud you
let this nightness safe you
this terrible sight of being pierces me with its acid iris of reality;
forcefed on adverts i didn't think people suffered anymore
But
now i know.
for i have seen hands clutch invisible gods at the blue of night
and
i have seen breath scatter sadness across once childrenned rooms;
i have seen death living
and living dying
in the parchmented lungs spitting out time
of flesh pinned to the bed by morphinned laces
allowing no escape from my sight
i have seen days shed silence into weeks / souls rise to
ceilings/voices fade to mute and i   i   i
am at a loss to explain.
if i were to paint cancer i would splash red and black resin upon a
white canvas and let it drip and clash like oceans of oil-
if i were to act cancer i would curl into a ball and close my eyes-
if i were to sing cancer i would scream until i tore my throat to a
million scagged shreds of severance-
if i were to describe this terrible honesty i would ask you to look
into her eyes
they tell no lies
they only tell;

But within the candle is the wick and
within/without
above/below
the cancer there lays the spirit
a spirit of suffering
a spirit sublime
this colossal caught sunflower speared by sun   yet
diminshed by time
a spirit of dignity denouncing
a spirit of humility hanging
this inside of pain this outside of smile
spirit how are you so strong in this unbearable bearing this
this
this
eternal trial?
and
beneath hymnned eyes brittle elbows and cancercracked skin
i have seen death
But
i   i   i
have seen life
of a serene soul/a dying body wept by our load
but the spirit is laying in the calm breeze of a childhoodhidden
road through the grass
glancing a meaning
a meaning at last
of a lucidity from reality a poem a life
this
terrible honesty
and i know
that
the brightest star is the deepest scar
the brightest star is the deepest scar

the deepest scar
is our brightest
b   r   i   g   h   t   e
s   t

star.

philosophy (father)
(for my father)

live small. think skies. hold others. deny yourself the luxury of
passivity. find contentment in asking questions. there are no
answers. no. no absolutes. understand that coming is but a
prelude to going. that then and if will always have a now. there.
there is no point in affluence. just another drug. affluence buys
you back. so. so continously strive for meaningful poverty. the
comfort of children's pictures. of autumn dawn. letterbox.
acknowledge the inked beauty born from struggle. alienation.
aloneness. despair. of tourniquets wrapped so tight your veins
recite epitaphs. epitaphs.
this hand upon hand. this letter upon letter. wound within
wound. this wish within why. this poem next to paint. this love,
this love stuttering to hate.
of
empathy.
rugged steel symphony. and this pen frightened of saying.
wisdom is not bought at marksandspencers. smallness is the
epitome of success. know the voice inside. watch the birds upon
rain telegraph wires. the failing. the failing candle.still.still.casts.
casts a shadow.
of angel.
ink.
solace.
whip.
work.
bled bleeding hands
of stone over soul and fuel within flesh.
so. lip another spectrum. another. another vocal chord.
the

eloquence
of
silence.
reaching.   torn.   into.
being.
of sadness. and as time   heaves its burden.
Just
like
the stars

we are   free

the   guerilla tapestry

"that is the secret and happiness and virtue-liking what you've
got to do. All conditioning aims at that; making people like their
inescapable social destiny"
brave new world

we
we are not deceived by your words
we see through your promises
we sanctify your lies
we
we are the disaffected
the isolated wounds of subtle napalm
shopping doesn't make us happy
commercials cull our sensitivity
freedom is nothing without responsibilty
and in these rain drenched tarpaulins of the market traders
is the epitome of belief
clinging to our pennies an entrance or exit
a memory or dream
this hole in my throat this gap in the ink
this place without meaning
this stuttering eloquence of screaming
so save
save us all
allow desolation
find a path
be unafraid to act
hold life
stand stand stand oak tall
even the smallest body makes a shadow

in the hanging out of washing
this protest of discipline
these tiny hands scraping solitudes clinging to moments
creating miracles from everyday routines
in the dignity of ironing
the anxiety of mortgages
the   the   the
sentence of being
but
still   still   still
the being
we are butterflies trapped in the frost
victory is acknowledging the fact that we
we
have not yet lost
so
caress me with your alienation
alienate me with your caress
create me with your credit
pour me power through direct debit
feed me freedom from selling shares
paint me a symbol and tell me i'm free
we   are
we   are
the guerilla tapestry
the silence of insurance payments
council tax benefits
industrial tribunals
the penny pinchers
the super savers
the lottery watchers
we   are
we   are

the incoherent throats searching for sound
the peaceful protestor
the separated father
the social worker at the homeless shelter
we   are
the happy shoppers
the credit cravers
the sales offers
poundstretchers
this breaking fabric of modernity
stitched only by our solitude
we   are
the temporary fragments of a capitalist master plan
unemployment statistics
family credit beggars
nocollarcoolies
part time slaves
sucking severances
praying for meaning
not this liplessened screaming
this atrophic sunrise
this pathetic attempt at remembrance
and in these motives that purify
in this act that dignifies
and in this tiny gesture of defiance
is an articulation of a void
of a vision versed in lament
this hate   this hate
is born from   love
we
we are the undying
the breath of chlorophyll over the concrete
we are loneliness burned

iron fists fuelled by injustice
we   are
the denied
yetunified
we are the tapestry
the crackling cracks of modernity
dislocated desperations stitched together
by the disparate verses of our skin
i write therefore we exist
we exist therefore i write
and from this page this scream
this no
from the supermarket to the dole
from the youth centre to the old people's home
is the sound of
the alone to the alone
the sound the silence the sound the silence
of the ability to resist
and in this ink there is the blood of a thousand miners
the eyes of 500 dockers, the loneliness of 6000 steelworkers
the hearts of 58 refugees
the struggle of my father
the sensitivity of my mother
and the hands of my children
and in this prison cell there is the skysunlight
and in these words the power they try to deny us
the stab of a killer
the tourniquet of a nurse
and in this ink is
one
is
many
is you and i

and in this voice
the milk of my mother
against   against
their droughts that smother
mother to man
woman to child
this guerilla tapestry spread nationwide
and in this division
there is a unity
and in this incision
there is a sanctity
and in this pale silent page
blisters a cacophony enraged
with the burn of generations
following the bullets of emancipation
we   are
we   are
the threads
we   are
we   are
the severance
we   are
we   are
the stitches
we   are
we   are
a no   in   search   of   a   yes
we   are
we   are
the breaking
we   are
we   are
the making

the blindbeginningtosee
we   are
we   are
the guerilla tapestry

in the shadow of the birds

i walk
unworthy of their wings
as words whip innocence
sin layers love
sunlight lightens loneliness
shadows
shelter incoherence
mornings   mornings of anxiety
alienation   of   atrophic   modernity
delicate bones
crackling humanity
pavements worn by
faltering fuelling footsteps
generation after generation
hate after hate
tremble after temble
beauty to the abbatoir
lips to the cosmetic
i walk
resembling
iodine
worshipping motrin
frightened of feeling
from this ritalinned meaning
of a throat silence stitched though seeing
a cacophony of simplicity
voice of poppies
memory of metal
a million hours spent watching the skies
and still
i cannot remember what colour it is;

In the shadow of the birds
we are nothing
blanked out references
useless noise   aimless aims
we   will   never   fly
greed nails us to the ground
materials mould rituals restrict
insensation our altar;
the ties of lies
forever impaled upon the corpse of gravity
brain braindeadened-
in the shadow of the birds   i   walk

the first night on earth
(to ethan and evan)

and from this night filled emptiness
comes the harp of day
and out out out to this world
a tiny spark of light
a purity unfurled
this simplicity bringing light
here
begins a stream
unfolds a petal
altering reality to a dream
a rainbow out of the oilslick
a dolphin against the nets
all the tension anxiety and hate i am soon to forget
as he slips and curls cries and clings
as his breath blows away all money and diamond rings.
oh life a clean heart is beating here tonight
oh life a remembrance is forging the future.
I think there must be a god a something
to create this whole perfect thing
because out of all the wounds of this modernity
there here everywhere
there flames a bloodbirth of beauty and innocence
amidst the chaos
within this nothingness
begins

Begins
an everything
beginneth here our daily bread

oh lord make us not dead
beginneth here the poor and the giving
faith and healing
forever and ever
amen
A   Man-
the first night on earth
in
this
moment
i remember
all the other nights
all the other babies that shone into this world in such
nightsunlight
and i think of all their days spent crying
spent
waiting/watching
for signs in the sky and the shadows of guns
i think of them
i think of them
all the dereliction and despair
all the bombed out faces in bosnia
all the fearfilled streets children in guatemala
all the homeless across neoned cities
all the gas charred victims of hitler
all the starved eyes of Africa
All the Loneliness Aching and Injustice
all of this world
captured in a needle point of light
channelled to stick into my veins
and inject me with awareness
as my baby cries
nothing moves

(Everything Feels Forever)
under the grey glaring skies
a lip caught in frost
a tear   a care   a plea
for all that this world has lost
a baby cries
the whole world cries
the constant language of humanity
this image
this now
this everlasting clock tick

i cannot forget/i fumble for threads of connection
and
embark upon humanhood
overflowing with love yet disgusted by life
Here begins Existence
a baby's cry probes my apathy
i rise like steam
i feel like roses
a baby's cry
i remember why
i am a birth
a human
a Nothing
a baby cries on the first ngiht on earth.
i think i understand now
across the world
into our Hearts
throughout the Night
glittering us Light

the Father's hands are holding
the Mother's milk is pouring
pouring

pouring
from the past
imagining a future
Darkness is where the Stars are
as tonight a baby cries
thinkinghopingpraying
that this night will mould the rest
remembering all the other babies that were ever born
immaculate in their moment.

Loss is where i get my Spine
so find some Meaning Here
hear-

the father's hands are holding
the mother's milk is pouring
let the whole world drink
Tonight
she is not woman
and i am not man
we are
Human

oh lord

Let There Be Days Worthy of this Night

this night.

hiraeth

land of my father what have we done to you
as i look upon these valleyed streets
these stained silent streets of satellite suns that salaciously stare
as i walk these epiphanies of denigration and despair
to live in wales
is to be forever aware
of death-
it is here   there
everywhere   but nowhere
as i stare
at the liposuctioned values and created needs
as chapels close
and spars boom on sunday rained nights of nothingness
as i stare
at these corpse ridden streets of carpet warehouses
poundstretched days lottery dreams and woolworthed wants
we wear our work like leprosy
toshiba   touching toes
aiwa   trapping minds
lg   lacerating dignity
call centres   collapsing community-
factory fucked days spent under the clock of dreaming
grateful just to have a job
in production line economics   money made automatics
so we
struggle to survive
survive to struggle
freedom a credit card spree
is work, are our lives ever free?
so we

buy more feel less
feel less we buy more
we are
atrophy decorated with junk
hands holding a currency of illusion
mouths moving a mind incision
i am nothing
and no thing is
land of my children
what can we do for you?

the eloquence in the screaming

still
i know no
thing
all i retain all i articulate is the screaming
the frantic wrenching screaming
from the faces from the throats from the cathode from the
pain from this hate into this love;
but within the catheter borders of the screaming
lays a dripping dying crying eloquence
a terrible vociferation of every soul
we enclose within ourselves;
i retain
i feel a searing eloquence within
of words bathed in barbed wire
echoing in windowless rooms
pages in a grandfather's deathdrawer
leaves in a tornado vacuum,
these are the screams within
these these are the life streams bleeding from skin
for without the screaming there is
no
thing;
and if only you could know what i know
and if only i could know what you know
we could replace the without within
there is no eloquence without the screaming.

this mask i wear pours draughts down my throat
as deliquent thoughts are culled before they can breath
in this reasoned rationed technocracy

an otherness imposed upon from outsideness
inside
i am a bayonet
a volcanic ulcer of expulsion
yet i go nowhere
layered by fear
tarnished by tears
lays the stuttering voice of denial
the silenced dream of action
veining my mind like cocaine
lonely as a hurricane
blinding my eyes with hatred
of myself for i am not;
inside
the placid flesh
a needle ripping for release
feeling for the yellow core of dying beauty within;

silence-

bares the cursed child of freedom
the eloquence in the screaming
through pale corridors of routine
rituals wither sunflower sun
bending like old men at the crack of whip work
we shallow we collapse we consume
to soothe the dereliction
we sit,
we sit like ferns in stone
waiting to sleep -

pouring whitewash into our mouths
the delectable drenching of our souls

by the veneer of illusion
strangling the seed before the sun
can caress the latent power of this lip creation
breathing in alienation
across this factory floored nation
into our minds for more
the white disease-

for more

the belt the greed the maggot the money magic seed
of destruction and defraction
into us it comes
replacing our sad eloquence with the obscene apathy of
" have a nice day it could be you forget it all in an instant he was
killed by friendly fire of collateral damage and business relations"
a language of distraction
smothering the screaming with the businessed smile the teacher's
pen and the credit sale
seeping into the victims of the lobotomised caress
the destruction of the screaming
to make the place seem cleaner
is the grin of the corporater
the pen of the advertiser
the mouse of the banker

BUT

between the billboard masturbation
across highways of metallic isolation
there

there lives the deafening screaming of you me us
wiping out the diseased pages of apathy
that bleed our eloquence
with words of amnesia
that forgets the feeling
that chokes our resistance
and
here
there rises the blood of the trees
the blue of the dolphins
the spine of the mountains
the tongues of the tied
arise
arise
a hate eloquence and destroy the death dreaming
and
out there
in there
somewhere
is where
here
there
i desire to speak;
somewhere without limits and fences
sometime without tenses
i
desire
to speak

to

speak:

reach

and nothing is perfection
holes
fill
everything
hands fasten in mind distance;
aloneness the companion we cling to
when flesh fails.
if only
only if
repeat
recite
dissonance
of a world unfit for this living.
how
do we signify
what makes contact mean
if and wish constantly recoil into how;
and i cannot find the place for it
it will not enter the space for it.
the
violation
of the one
is the isolation of the two
yet the clock stutters sadness
and time oceans along
indifferent to the apostate of hearts
that once bled together
now stab each other
so
nail hope to the bandage

crush fracture into flowers

can.
can
belonging
ever
belong

again?

11:11:11

listen,
two minutes silence in a century of screams
the rain pours
the poppy will not flower
the flesh bleeds
upon memory
no peace in flanders fields
no rest for saro-wiwa
just the sound of history's necrophilia
and metal detectors scraping sacred soil

you are steel
you are bullet
you are blood
you are broken
and i,
i am a remembrance forgotten
on an antiseptic morning in london
i am a cenotaph souvenir stall selling
you are not

listen,
listen and you will hear
two minutes silence in a century of screams -
no heartbeat to confirm existence
only the bled arteries upon Time
only the white flag deathdrugged and mindunmanmade
from calvary to chechnya
frombethlehem to bosnia
from the somme to the falls road

a bloodfeast of death symphony
a mindfast of sympathy
and as we bow our heads in prayer
listen,
listen
and you will hear
two minutes silence in this century of screams.

christmas lights in january

rain beat my soul
empty me in
drizzling distances heart sedated
isolations
isolate
and dignify
as

tears
come to signify
a defiance
a shroud
a loss
a dolphinned silence
of uninterrupted eloquence.

strung out like eyes
cold as worship
bleeding blood colour over sun denied streets
they
watch
they
wait
like Jesus upon Calvary

to be
dragged down
and
put away

until
until

another
sense
of
belonging

occurs.

memoria

there is springtime in death
the wind punished grass cannot be halted
as even in choking there is breath;
the flowers that bloom
are the flowers of pain
in sadness/ in hate/ in defiance/ in despair/
they stab the soil in silence with their chroma hymns
they, they shall remain
across parchment deserts and money stained streets
in morphinned bedrooms of illnesslessened bodies
through cracks in the ink
the ravaged rainbow bleeds through.

against the bloodstained canvas of calvary
the petals/the leaves/the bulbs/
the mind paints its colour / its renewal
into our lives
though there is a cross
trees still shelter
though bullets replace nails
crucifixion still occurs

there shall be doves
there shall be doves;

in this
blood within wound/flesh over nails/sky above man/weep into
why
placenta through death
in memory /in hope/ in hurt/ in plea/

there are seeds planted daily
even though then is pain
today today
shall have a tomorrow
there is springtime in death
there is prayer in sorrow
though yesterday burns
today
today shall have a tomorrow

democratis

you sinn fein fascists
serb sadist
welsh nationalist
force feeding paramilitary
clinging to your ideology
freedom without responsibility
necrophilia your calling card
you hold no salvation
only hatred injustice and oppression
hitler your omniscient bard

there is no unity in one langauge
no compassion inyour petrol bombs
your education is brain damage
fists your fuel ignorance your blame
japan says sorry enola gay is celebrated history
redemption is won territory
you kill to live
you chain to free
orange men white man
croat ss
belsen gas
religion slits wrists
while belief burdens bodies
of aryan ethic
soul laceration
bullets your emancipation
ss sas ira cia uda mia raf usa uk
cut up/ divide / destroy/ deny/
all manifestos breed segregation

all wars intoleration
your violence
no redemption
no redemption.

their life on their heads

"In a crowd of over 10,000 refugees sprawled over Tuzla's cornfields, a young woman hanged herself yesterday. No one knew her name. No one wept for her when her body was cut down from a tree, and only a single bored policeman kept vigil over the corpse as it lay abandoned by the gate of the heaving sweating camp"

The Guardian July 14th 1995

and we watch
and we watch in our safe homes through marks and spencered curtains
at the unfolding of another   another celluloid
tragedy
upon insensate sofas feeling sorry for ourselves that we can't quite
afford that new house or envious of next door's carpet
peering through tunnel visionned lenses at the tv screen;
responding   robotic   rituals
of;
"how terrible-how sad-aren't we lucky-what time is home and away on?"
until it's time to sleep   until it's time to sleep-
we observe, painless puritans pretending to care
we watch   we switch off
we watch   we switch off
then we fall back to our usual apathy and comforted routines and lives
as
humanity self immolates like sandcastles upon a beach
the water drowns while we sip evian and remove our facial mask;

through the cathode feed we suck celluloid
stare   stare   at the tv   tvpeople
as millions starve
only needing the basics   we blatantly avoid
in our pathetic attempt to exist while they walk aeons
on incarcerated feet across deserted deserts and desperate streets
only freedom and peace they ultimately seek;
and under this westernised sun
the glare of ozonelessened yellow
that stains their skin   that chokes their throats as flies
settle on week old babies
no mother no father to cling   to no other
but this milk drought of breasts bleeding from this world's sin
and we watch
and i wish someone would cover my eyes
i wish someone would make us see
their life on their heads
a bundle of the past
a complete incompleteness
a future fading fast
their life on their heads
a diet of nothingness
a few grains of rice
a handful of water
dripping dragged from each other's tear bledbleeding eyes
while we we we
choose plastic surgery to remove our third chin
they, the tv people walk like cancer shedding their skin
and so we watch the tv
voiceless voyeurs   inactive activities
we munch our plastic then liposuck the fat
and we watch   we switch off
we watch

this unreal reality
watchingeatingsleepingwatching
untouchable people weeping impotence into our living rooms

tv   people   what is real?

tv   people   feel the scream   scag my throat
tv   people   cannot touch

tv   people

them   or   us

themorus?

scalpelandheart

your five fingers growing
beneath this star stemmed sky   and
into the mindlight of anxieties
the moon whispers its words across our silence
entering an everything with verbs of nothing

your five fingers growing
against a crow sky
into this barcoded daylight
that drowns our questions
your five fingers growing
flesh filling flesh
fragile bones bearing witness
sucking/holding/clutching rainbows
my hands are emptiness when compared to this

so how can i tell you
that fingers pull a trigger
that hands make a fist   smash jaws
push buttons
hold knives to extinguish a belief in this life/living/live?
how can i hold you with such adulterated palms and lipsilenced
values
when man culls man
for religion   for love   for nothing-

your five fingers growing
attuned to gentleness   cloud   and star
pink miniatures of man
with without this blood bleeding;

and i stare, i stare at your fragile fingers that fuse
how they reach and hold
how they search and ask
how they balance   in air   in sleep
harming nothing
hurting no one
only knowing
the breeze and the breath of brothers and sisters
your touch of harmlessened fingers of fractured foreverness
and so   as night smoothes your eyelids and
sleep slips into skin
i hold your hand   and count my   fingers

dysunitednation

"everyone has the right to seek and to enjoy in other countries
asylum from persecution"
article 14 of the universal declaration of human rights

in great great britain
land of hope and glory
land of the fucking fairy tale story
patrol your borders obey their orders
spend 563 million on the dome
but close our hospitals and moan
at asylum seekers taking our money
our homes our jobs our liberty
let's lock 'em up before they destroy our economy
"ssssseeeeeeeeeee
we're loveleee people we ain't no racists
but if you cum yer you'll get ower fists"
in great great britain
built on workingclass sweatandblood
and oh i almost forgot on cambridge and oxford
this dysunited nation of red white and blue
of white male bigotry and children learning thru
sun headlines and telegraphed lies
hague proclaims blair denies
as 58 refugees die in front of our eyes
patrol your borders obey their orders
but we welcome hitachi aiwa toshiba and lg
we worship ginola zola and vialli
yet we spit,
we spit at frightened refugees
so;

i propose that next time a politician or anybody mentions the
words detention and refugee
i will ask them to look in my bible -
the dictionary
where they will see that refuge is before refugee
and detente comes before detention
so-

ignore their orders destroy all borders

ignore their orders destroy all borders;

crucifixion2000

blood   resilence
        hope   neglected
race   burning
purity   embraced   like   comm e rc   e
wood   lipped
plastic coffinned
blood bled   days singing
holygreen   indifference
carved by money
electric hymns   paid by credit card
        boutique
            onwardchristiansoldiers
        trampled bibles jehovahed eyes
scanning sadscorched earth
blood tranfusion   this humanity
a sanctity of saline
failing
to immerse   minds eternally
in
the-

nails   nowhere
blood   everywhere
skin only d e to   xed by   death
care   ful-
a
dyeing word from a desperate mouth
more
more
MORE:

truthdemanded

i shall be bread,   beginning
i shall be wine,   waiting
i shall be all the things in decline

within this place
out of this face
i shall rejoice
the blood that pours
the flesh that scars
shall be my mind forever last
amongst the debris
between the pain
is a trapped nerve feeling all that remains
between the poem and the bullet
lives the dignity and the despair
holds the bones together while the sadness tears

dust specks
insect bites
inside lips
an eternity
unafraid to walk humanly
2000 years and what have we learnt
computer modems can't communicate the hurt
we stumble stutter and crawl
an unholy communion birthed from greed as
blood pours ligaments split tongues jabber
e-religion the silent lifesaver?
we came we saw we shopped
chocolate eggs won't halt the death we want

daffodils dance lambs litter the fields
sunday prayers as zimbabwe burns
the whiteblack sun is deafening
the silence showers our silence

we are bread,   breaking
we are wine,   bleeding
we are the living dead
dying, dying

BEGINNING:

of temazepam and petroleum

in;
the sky's reflection
splinters into vodka puddles
a lippedpetrol smear upon adolescent   tarmac-

upon;
these tortured sidewalks and hilfigered limbs
a litter of language spilled from lagered tongues

fuckyoucoolasfuckmunwankerwhosaengoanen go on-

so you blank it out you burn it out

of;
acetylene hum of testosterone and
alcopopped   eyes
scanningsulphur   streets
staring   staring   staring

laptopsoftopturboburstcheckshirtoutside
-i wear my umbro jacket though i've never kicked a ball in
mylife-

CAR TRAP BEHIND SHUTTERS
a MECCA of aluminium cadence of stopped clocks
IT COULD BE you IT COULD BE you
of jungle beats   mind halts
and acid drops
dripping
dripping

from a starwished   sky
of an ironlunged corridor of   whylesswant
and trade
fed by disease and decadence
dancing dancing dancing
in;

the sky's reflection

and what are you wales?

an
other
statistic
an
other petalled sympathy another joyrider another drug victim
another factoria another soul
rising rising rising
to the stars above.
we.
we are the fallen the un the dis the in the lost people
we commune with the ghosts of forever upon chapelled
breaths.acned faces pushed tight against mortuary glass staring
staring at the sun-
my son   my son.
prozac ain't no bandage to this much blood.
bleeding. bled. it could be you doesn't necessarily mean winning
the lottery
we.
we are holy.we are epiphany.we are full of holes.
holes.holes.holes.
adverted smiles.daz whiteness.hollywood dreams and and and
rhymneyed nights.   silence.
sil   ent stone mountains
greygreat skies staring.staring.
of migrained malls dead workingmen's halls.
holding.holding.holding
our lottery numbers like genitals
bowing to workingclass wankers on golden pedestals.
so.design your life.burn your flag.live the green.plead for blood.
hold.

heal.

faith.

feeling.

fury

      feel.
an
other.   another.

weep for centuries

the poignancy of regret
holes to be filled
gaps to be immersed in air
breathing. breathing to be resumed
all that we are
nowhere.
all that we were
everywhere.
night air
vodka and piss
lay-by highs and diazepamed dawns
of now and then
then
forever
everfor
this.   live
remember this   remember   this
neon decay
searching souls   everlasting footsteps
remain

remain

remain

in
the
foetal

p   o   s   i   t   i   o   n.

demonstrations for existence

a.the unification

"I won't call it a strike. I would call it a demonstration for
existence...........the miners in South Wales are saying, "we are
not accepting the dereliction of our mining valleys, we are not
allowing our children to go immediately from school into the
dole queue. It is time we fought."
Emlyn Williams 1981

tomorrow

filed away into the redtaped self assurance of office regulations
newlaboured toried amnesia
of the gutwrenched days of dust and blackened blood-

this be the verse of commemoration

of
swallowing servility
spitting out dignity
making miracles from everydayed work in the belief of a better
place
through education
from a blacked out face
for emancipation
of a solaced smile
from walking underground miles
of creating a life to be
of communal obligation

of paying for the books in the library

this be the verse of commemoration

through the lies of this fucking century
first
thatchered denial of our fragiled history
now
blair
sits in socialist splendour
ignoring this struggling community
YOU
can call it politics
blind us with statistics
starve us with your economics
lie to us with your campaign rhetoric
loud hail about your humanity
BUT
now   now   now

today

as the breathing blisters and lungs cough black
you imprison us with the degrading foreign factory
preach to us about common decency
but as
the eyes and hands that wait for the post to drop
but what about fucking morality
£6000 for a life underground?
your silence is like bedwellty cemetery
but without the stuttered dignity
without the sense of urgency
of 80,000 souls waiting to be heard

this -   this has to stop

and   as

tomorrow

breathes through the green haze of an oxygen mask
let us remember the mountained fresh

yesterdays

of labour, family, dignity and meaning
and let us,   through
these voices
these truths
these histories
these eyes
these lungs
in unity   in hope   in disgust
exhale
and
let them hear HERE our screaming
let decency prevail
and allow

today   today   today

to be to be TO BE

still breathing

still   breathing -

tomorrow
to;   tomorrow

demonstrations for existence

b. selling smiles

"what one must seek is integrity and vitality- one's holy grail is
the living truth, knowing that being alive the truth must change"
Aneurin Bevan

smile
serve
smile
see
earn
burn
be
smile
serve
see
save save save
grave grave grave
but
made made made
in
wales.
wales.wales.
as fragments of dignity
invade our speech invite william hague
to dig a plot
come to wales and get a job
m4 corridor you're not out of reach
so sell me a smile and tie me to the line
make me piss my pants

but get an nvq in making tea
aiwa toshiba hitachi
pyrrhic factories
surrogate mines
a stuttered sense of liberty
so
cellulite my valley
silicone the economy
cross breed fertility
leave behind mind sterility
so
sell me a smile
come to wales and save and smile and serve
and
be
and
see
stare
at
the
sun
and
squint
your
eyes
smile
and
serve
freedom equality and emancipation
no obligation
indelible abrasion
is welsh
for profit-

nothingland

ONCE WE WERE NOW WE ARE
toll on our personal lives shall i call an ambulance claimline 0800
can you?
SALES OFFERS DOT COM TAKEOVERS
do something hurts in accidents doctor doctor too fast slow
down slow down   can you?
BORDER PATROLLED SOULS
choice is bigger when catch foot and mouth for years and years
UNLIMITED LIMITS
the roses can take care of themselves from kitchen and
bathrooms we
AK47 CREDIT CARD EPIPHANY
got no brain to carry everything on your back you gotta
WE WALK THE WORLD ON THE INTERNET/SWALLOW
WHOLE
just try   can you?
DAYTIME TV
FUCK BABIES THEN PRAY FOR FORGIVENESS ON
JERRY
SEE IT ALL HAVE IT ALL FORGET IT ALL
FOR AN INSTANT
CHOOSE YOUR AMPUTATION
PAY FOR YOUR DEGRADATION
A SICKLE CELL EDUCATION
good good vibrations looktotomorrow the real ira have claimed
REFUGEE/CATTLE TRUCK/FREEDOM/WORM
INFESTATION
SELF REVERED/RELIGION OF/ THE NEW
EMANCIPATION
FOOT AND MOUTH OUTBREAKS

AND GUERILLA ATTACKS
IODINE DENIED
UNDERSTANDING FEIGNED OR CRUCIFIED
YOU AND ME ME AND YOU US AND THEM WE AND I
WILL NEVER SEE EYE TO EYE
SO WE PLUCK THEM OUT
A SILENT APOCALYPSE
FROM FEARFILLED LIPS

WE SEE NOTHING
WE HEAR NOTHING
WE FEEL NOTHING
WHILE EVERYTHING CRIES AND EVERYTHING DIES
SO GIVE ME MY TAX RELIEF ON MY DEAD OF
COVENANT CHARITY DONATION
BOW DOWN, KNIGHT ME, SHOW SOME
APPRECIATION
A PARAMEDIC POLEMIC
A NARCISSISTIC EPIDEMIC
OF DISCIVILIZATION
IN NOTHINGLAND/EVERYTHING BREAKS
IN NOTHINGLAND/EVERYBODY TAKES
now news of profit growth and
A SPLENDOUR OF SELF BANDAGES THE MANY
A METHADONE ASSEMBLY SEARCHING FOR SANCTITY
A GLOBAL CATASTROPHE BEGINS AT HOME
the disease is not present but new supplies are making it to the
shops minister would you please answer the question
IT'S MORE THAN THE SHEEP WE'VE CLONED
CHOKE SLAM MY MIND
CARVE YOUR CRACK UPON MY NECK
IN THIS SELFOCRACY OF THE BLIND
the mortgages of

IN NOTHINGLAND   EVERYTHING GOES
prize money available
THIS FETISH OF FORGETFULNESS
A MESS OF FLESH
THIS PROZAC WILDERNESS
THIS VIAGRAED SPACE SPARKLING
THIS NECROPHILIAC KISS
THAT STINGS
THIS COPROPHILIA OF THE SOUL
THAT CLINGS
IN NOTHINGLAND   NOTHING GROWS
one person was deemed responsible
AND SO WE WALK
AND SO WE WALK.
standard fares only at this time of day
A HISTORIED LACERATION
it's a high quality finish and will not be beaten on choice or price
with the wider rim it appears more versatile
OF VIRTUAL ISOLATION
THE INSTANT GRATIFICATION A KIND OF
ANAESTHESIA
TO BLANK OUT THE GREYING OPPRESSION
SO FACE LIFT THE PAIN
EYES STILL THE SAME
the benefits of air you'll get that tingling sensation
IN NOTHINGLAND
THE DROWNING DAYS DARKEN
or your money back phone now on
DRAGGING FEET UPON SUICIDE BEACH
RAGGED CLOTHES ON PETRIFIED BACKS
INSIDE THE APPLE MAGGOTS CRAWL
WITHIN THE SOUL WORMS SWARM

more successful more productive
PESTILENT AIR OF INVISIBLE WAR
THE SCARS WE ARE
THE DANCE/ THE DELIRIUM/ THE DYING
THE MUCK OF MAMMON MARKING
THE FIST OF FUCKING HITTING
THESE ARE THE DROWNING DAYS
LIVING SMALL IN MANNEQUIN LAND
COMPANY CRASH FINANCIAL NEED
I'VE LISTENED TO AUTOMATED HELP LINES
UNTIL MY EARS BLEED
£5 for one £12 for 2
you can
you can
I'VE STAYED SILENT FAR TOO LONG
THIS MOUTH TOO STARVED TO FEED
I'VE SEEN THE MOUNTAINS CRUMBLE
I'VE SEEN THE CHILDREN STOOP
BLEACH ONLY CRAVES THE DIRT LIKE THE NECK,
ROPE
a puff of smoke a blade of grass here today gone tomorrow
LIPOSUCTION CAN ONLY REMOVE WHAT WAS NEVER
THERE
LIKE
NOTHINGLAND
thy will be done
you can you can
I WHICH I NEVER WAS
thy will be done
john 21 verse 2
you can   you can   YOU CAN   you can
ONCE WE WERE
the beauty of submission

the beauty of su-

NOW WE ARE

WE ARE.

heartwork

but
behind ache
we place
garden in sleep to recall
one moment under music we sing/
dream/
truly
of   on   to
love
falling go going gone go
but

whispering

wanted   still   always

a diamond our
was here
and
let sky incubate
our footsteps
and
think
never
there-

wanted   still   always;

the unsaid

autumned nights

know
of the
torn wrist
b
l
e
e
d
      ing
undercovers
the bloodshot eye
staring
      at the orangelit glow of
3 am
of
rain and leaf

l   e   a   v   i   n   g

left /gone/ severed/sentenced/sold/

of autumnednights of viagraed verses

versus

versus:

verse us

us

u   s-

thereisnoone   t(h   e   r   e)

mind cauterized
in
camouflage
rainwashed grass giving
respite
lips (always)
(lips)   always
silence and struggle
violence and silence
allowing
following
feeling
to

(be)   felt;
furious i hold the simplicity

f
a
l
l
i
n
g,

i fear the onset of next
and into out of within with insides like chalk circles carving out a
language
spitting out a remembrance
holding onto the damage

to (heal)
lips (always)
lips always
ending in
sucked silence

(silence)
the silents;

against
(for my children)

do not submit to the grey world
the grey world of grey faces in grey suits with greying thoughts
in greyed buildings of grey lives
do not allow your blue bluest bluer blue eyes cast grey looks into
the beautiful wildness of your dreams
do not let the fake green their grey green
corrode your truth green
the green of fields of smiles of chlorophylled lips and
summerlicked meadows
do not let the greygreen gods of
envy lust money and greed
corrupt your mountainthoughts
your fieldvision and your rivereddreams
that
shall last forever
forever last
as long as your hearts shall
beat
beat
with the rainbowravaged song
of chromaed childhood belief

do not submit to their grey my loves

their grey ways my loves

my loves;

Nobodaddy
(for clive payne & mark harris)

"90% of all homeless and runaway children are form fatherless homes and 60% of youth suicides are from fatherless homes"

tell us how we talk
tell us how we dress our children
tell us how much we have to pay you
tell us how pathetic a father we are
tell us how our children don't want to come with us
tell us what to buy them for christmas
tell us we are failures
tell us
tell us
tell us what time we have to pick up our children
the children we used to carry on our shoulders in timeless pride
and beautiful moments
the same children we have nurtured and fed awoke to their every
call and cry - bled our minds into total oblivion because of love
now we long now we stutter - afraid of your clocks your
prescription of behaviour your normality of objection
relinquish your entitlements dig your dogma as you destroy ours
as
now we walk head stooped watching through the cracks in the
playground wall-
now
you bastards
how dare you reduce us to nothings nothings
to a visitor a contact a saturday afternooned father a frightened
noun of crowned obsolescence

"be there at five
don't give them sweets
don't iron pyjamas
i wish you would hit me so that i could get an injunction against
you
i regret the day i let them call you dad-"
dad   dad   dad;
we accuse
weaccuse
w   e   a   c   c   u   s   e

its time you listened-listened;

"the last time i spoke to my four year old daughter was 10 days
ago and it's been two months since i last saw her. I'd waited all
night for her to call. When it finally came, after chatting away
gaily for a few minutes she came out with the words........daddy i
don't love you anymore"
*clive payne on a recent phone call from his daughter in new
zealand.*

*mark harris was imprisoned for 10 months for breaking a court
imposed order preventing him from seeing his children.*

scardust

crawling to stand standing to crawl
crushed little fucker stuck to the sound
of beetle trapped underground
loving caring father hoping feeling son
why is that you make my heart so fucked up
we
all alone face each day as wound
face each breath with anxiety no self help book can cure
cannot speak cannot think everything inside curls and clings to
moments of meaning
to the insides dying to the beautiful selfsacrifice of
screaming-
the silence of silence the torment of torment the no of no
the knowing of knowing
so
run hide smile sleep
crushed little fucker don't get too deep
drowning in your aridity
thirsty in your ocean
cold in your climate
frightened of your comfort
holding onto your distance
dancing inyour shadow
this loneliness i shall keep
and embroider it into my flesh
slit the throat to speak
place it in my thorax
crushed little fucker
remind myself i'm not

to weep-weep
to-

screams find ears in the loneliest of places
screams find ears in the loneliest of places

thebreaking

black/ lips/ speaking/ white/ lies/
licking /narrow /corners/ of/ desperate/ mouth/
face/ contorts/ into/ schizophrenic/ electric/
silence/ of/ sharing/
the /sharing/ of/ silence/
shards/ the/ shawl/
we/ cut/ to/ wrap/
inside/ each/
each /inside/
a /cancer/ cracking/
a
whole into   holes
a /feeling /fallen/
an emptiness drowning
a then
whenned
into
now

no;

1 million blankets

1 million blankets given out during the kosovo conflict in 1999
the 6 billionth baby was recently born

to cover the world's pain
to warm the world's cold
to to to to
soak the world's blood
1 million blankets
shelter our frightened children
through the adulterated night
so put your hands beneath the covers
close your eyes
do not cry
for the tears freeze upon your lips
speak to the sky the beautiful breaking blue sky
above,
let the blanket shoulder the pain
let it drain
of all colours
flags emblems languages skins weapons anthems
onto
one flesh
undesignated uncountried deflagged and silent
yours and our flesh
one million blankets
in fields in mountains in doorways
in concrete
under the spiteful rain
beneath
the scorchingsun

upon the bloodsoaked snow
within
our atrophic hearts
these blankets know no borders
shelter stutters through words
words fucking words
can you hear them can you can you???

blanket bombing/ blank it out/blanket bath/ bloodblanket/
birthblanket/blanket of snow
blank out what you know
safety blanket/
fire blanket/
your blanket/
my blanket   our blanket
that covers our sins
indelible upon our skins
still they scream
scratched flesh no dreams
one million blankets
hide/safe/warm/clothe/care for/
this bloodless crucifixion
under the staring skies
that still sparkle
of sadness and despair

united by the blankets
yet torn by our language
lipped by our tongues
yet tortured because of our skins
one million blankets and 6 billion souls to save

1 million blankets

but   it i s s   t   i ll   socoldhere

so cold here-

so cold

so?

adrenalined

eclipsed
buried born from birth
stop
hold   and   heal
have
not   possess
purify
deify   cannot
can't   believe
belief
burn burnburn   burn
bebebe   be   be b   e
satisfy
memorify
unify
walk upon the beach
stare at the sky
hold a moment
eclipse
eclipsed
/
-behind
          some   moment
light wewhisper

under
elaborate   skin
of
only mist
ache/ache;

the in-shining

children asleep
2 a.m.
in slowslumbered sanctity

no stitches to hold them together
no pills to help them sleep
no injections to detox their flesh
no flotation tanks to calm their minds
no health club vistas
no jogging machines
no heart rate testers
no lo cal handsfree go ahead it could be you maybe
sweetener free
low e
content
high fibre
traces of sodium
buy 1 get 2 points loyalty card mind manipulations

NO:

just these hands
these eyelids
under these stars
in
this breeze that blows
and this head
that hurts
trying to steady itself

bowing

before,

before the candle stutters to sleep-

to sleep;

swan in sunlight
(for my mother)

on mornings such as this
i wonder what it was like
when you were born
shone into this world like a sparkle
and
wonder how you played and ran
sang
and grew into
what made me

on mornings such as this
i see you in silent splendour
a swan in sunlight
swimming in slow water
against a green world
the feminisation
of my
masculinisation
the tears in the eye of man
the fist unfurling to
hold,
to hold   to hold

on mornings such as this
all i can do
is write my mind upon paper
to speak of things that truly matter
and
to acknowledge a life

of care   beauty
and motherhood hidden from heroes
on mornings such as this
i see you shine and sprinkle stars forever
a swan in sunlight

gliding
gliding
gliding......................

nowhereland

distance
drips
computer screen
blinks
children delicately
sleep
the sleep of beauty born
untarnished untorn
as
we stamp like stones into the oblivious night
night -
as nothing normals this disaffection
we pour desperation into days
dragging out the dead embryos of yesterday
bleeding
bleeding
so easy to blame so easy to scream
so easy to say nothing at all
so hard to fall
i've never been afraid of much
but now the verb

going

stabs my stomach and stammers my tongue
crunches my crescend into dispersal
of thoughts to depraved solicitude
of of of and into out of into with you without you
now i stand or do i crawl
a cranial withdrawal

this mental dislogical wall
that walls us in
over which the fingertips
grip then split
grip then split
like blood bled from diseased skin
within
with in
which
we
we cannot fit within
with   out
with-

sanctorum number one

the flowers that grow
from the lips that cease
the todays that tear the throat
from tomorrow's speech
the space between
into
out of
within
within
the moments eternally melting
into the internalled resurrection
of yesterday
letters upon a stone
fragments of a life
prematurely torn
from this earthed desolation
still
still
too soon the knife
too late the words
wishing summer never came
wishing everything could be the same
and in the silent fields
the flowers that grow
though the lips have ceased
in colour corroded chroma
stamen simplicity
of carvedcalm cacophony
in

this undying
grassgrowing
peace
in this
flowerfed silence
that speaks so eloquently
the flowers still grow
though the lips have ceased
the flowers still grow;
still
grow-

to james monty and sue
july 2000

when we wake up today will it be tomorrow?
(evan jones august 2000)

will it
can it
ever
change
relinquish
free
to
to
be
ever
ever
to
ever
again
isn't
it
isn't
it
ever
ever?
if
we
can't
can
we
wake
up
ever

today
tomorrow
tomorrow
to
tomorrow
to;

to-

let your soul start
(ethan jones 2001)

icareformychildren
i wipe their cheeks
i cook them food
i smile at their jokes
i let them win
i always begin
i will not end
i am a dad
a father
unafraid to stand
to be feminine
in my masculine
to be masculine in my masculine
i shall not bow my head
i shall not close eyes
except to visualise my children
when they are away
then
but
now
i walk
head up to the wind
like trees stretching their chlorophylled necks to the sky
this sky my sky your sky

our sky

that will not die/that will not die

i   am   a   dad
i will be a dad
still still still
so still
i wait so still
still
i be
i am a dad
i will be a dad-
thisisjustthebeginning.

the daylight of the fading

this is my light
the daylit leftovers of pain
ingrained in emergent dark
hands forging out a path
this is how my smile slashes my pain
this is how my heart passes the beating,
this is how i shall walk
this is how i shall feel
broken verses believing
this is my light
the darkest darkness
the atrophic mind
waiting
the bled artery
healing
the stanley knife
cutting
the decaying marrow from this existence

this
this
is my light

lit;

lighting.

father's day 2000

today,
i walk head down neck beat mindworn shouldersnapped against
the vitrolic afterburn of unman
today
i do not know how to hold my head up for my gender
stare ahead - too cold
stare away - coward
cry   too feminine
hold back   egotistical

picture me in a frame
carbon me into you
xeroxed testosterone throated in derelict muscles
hold me in my history
pour me another malt whiskey will it make you smile
castrate me for the present
denote me my future
the femination of my realization
is my downfall
the prozacpulse of necrophiliac emancipation
to be
to be
to be

a
man
this man
now
today
who shakes inside at the soiled portrait that stares from celluloid

that spits from terraces
that imprisons feelings
that is afraid to be afraid
that is
i
only know
that it is easy
to become a father
but
so
much
harder
to be one;

exit holes

a sadness incurred sadness
upon truth trying days
within
you
momentary peace as sunlight upon
rainraged rooftops
shining
shining
through you
and what is this moment under this sky within this flesh
but the fallopian tube
of another
another
another
failed attempt at living
into me and out of me the injury swells
blood begins where the wound inhales
i can analyse the past
yet need to design my future
so full of holes.
holes so deep i can place my hand to grope and grutter the
slowing pulse of meanings moving in and out of consciousness
culling
corporeal angels bloat the spot of entry
the trigger of pain that survives the rip
into me and out of me run the words
sweet bile to blister a tormentor's tongue that twists and turns
away
delicate smiles to wilt the torpored days of atrophying apathy
inscape to escape

in shining we blind our enemies
in shining
shining in we see towards another light
lit
lips carrying light to another
another
an   other
carves my name in flesh
failing
forever the holes
holes of mercy
holes of loss
holes of painpetrified days
holes of night
holes that worship
holes that die
holes that guide
holes that deny perfection
holes that are the world's reflection
forever the holes
i exhalt the unseen stabs that we breathe
i exhibit openly to whoever asks i have no shame
i am made of holes
holes,
of shattered flesh and erased mind
i stand in such sunlight
my shadow is
engraved
my holes crusade
the holes of consciousness guide my hands
where prayers pretend
my holes
heal

and hold the moments together like black masking tape
strapped together
undying
unseen
holes
that fuse
this
life
holes
that create
the whole/whole;

delirium in white silence
(for rebekah and victoria)

"In discussions about children's welfare the term parent still too easliy becomes a synonym for "mother". Traditionally women have been associated with the care and nurturance of children in ways never expected of me. The term "mothering" suggests a warm protectiveness, a uniquely feminine form of affection - in contrast "fathering" implies only begetting" *(Gittins-1985)*

dragging itself from the hook
to parry thoughts
like
suicide
words blaze in unspokened arteries
resilence of moments
melting
only
now
eternity stutters into the gap
the gap
that grows as it closes
don't know what to do - try to
busy myself with adult things
paint/ iron /read/ watch/ clean
when all i want to do is hear your voices in the room next door
all i want to do is wipe
your cheeks
all i want to do is tell you to be quiet -
pull your trousers up
tell you to eat your greens

and
and
and
and
wait for you to fall asleep
head wrapped against me
instead
i watch the red seconds tick
for hours
days
weeks
weak
am i?

it takes discipline to be this sad;

with the sense of an ending

still the mountain
still the walking
still the breathing
still the choking
still the cutting
still the bleeding
still the feeling
still the loving
still the clock ticking
still the leaf shaking
still the silence screaming
still the ink leaking
still
still
still
be
still
still
bestill
be
still
still
be
still
be; still -

the ending
still
still   this   this   still
be   beginning

such. natural. symmetry.

summer.park.sunlit.eyes.glint.
ending.day.opening.heart.
such.sky.such.souls.such togetherness.untorn.untimed.
wordsfromtonguesglide
like swifts in
summer.park.eyes.sunlit.me.watching.you.you.watching.me.us.
us

us

the vulnerability of the one shall outlast the victory of the masses

today the world is ugly
today the world throws bricks onto my bones
today the world bleeds
today the sky sharpens itself upon glass
today hepatitis B spits into my mouth
today i feel alone

i want it to shine
i want it to be clean
i want it to be meaning
i want to fit in

so i think of the moments
i think of the feelings
i think of the glittering
never too cynical to hold a hand
never too young to learn
always too bled to bleed
always too wept to weep
but we can sky the stars and let them in
we can remember the things that made us
we can hold the hands that created
lick the loss that divides us
pour the pain into petals let them grow
let the moments glisten like blood flow
let the memory dignify
only the beautiful things i will let in
all the beautiful things in me
only the beautiful things i cling to thee

the moments of meaning will not melt
the tarnish of time will not kill
the verses the visions of my incision
the elegance will remain

the image of you to sparkle
this darkness
only the beautiful things
is where we start from
from

here;

prototypes of human sorrow

we walk unseen through the starving eye
deluded and desperate
moneymade incarnate
untouching/touched too much by the vacuum that visions
tortured mannequins melting slowly
blindfolded fed saturation points
and so we walk,
stumbling lives in blinding light
we crave we create we cure the less by having more
we silent the voice that we need
for the viruswant of wishing when/
cancer comes takes friends away
hearts attack bring birthblood back
to age aloneness and decay
disease dances upon our despair
we seek solace in everything
but the simple things
darkness causes a search for light
cessation starts the awareness to cling
what is not craves to be once more
a minute a moment spent holding the hand of resilience
we amputated by money speed and indifference
we cling to the collapsing normality
of what once was
searching for what will never be
fingers scraping roses in silent cemetery
mouths moving minds of fearfilled insanity
of when in awe of then but no
if exists when the pain persists
and all we have left is a picture upon the bedroom wall

that asks to be left alone
this petrified purgatory
of isolated dignity
of a sense of time cracked stones
we belong we belong we belong
but in these hours spent watching the beautiful sky
how is it that i never remembered to ask why?
which is why we live - of course it is -
yet still the deaths haunt and life insists
we learn to die
we walk unseen through the starving eye
oh feed me feed me feed me
so i may try to remember all the souls i walk within
so my voice may speak   my ears listen
my heart give   and my mind receive the moments
that may piece together an eternity
from this fractured life we lead
we seek solace out of everything but the simple things
and it is these this now
to which we must cling
to which we must cling

cathedra

we must overcome this
we must move higher
clasp branches
hold firm
feel again
know again
real   (r) ise
real   ise
what we are were and will be
again
know
no
now
this pain can only exist upon the body
there must be a residing place
where one day
we shall be whole
in holes
again
again
for this time these days
the minutes stick like flies in honey
falling
uncompromising
unfeeling
unlistening
unhearing
un dis ir dys an de
everything starts with a negation
can something begin with an affirmation

a somewhered
verb of
unatrophied flesh
to heal
this
again
again;
we have to overcome this/

somewherelight

leaving   this   hole

filters
forges

fears

fills
t   h   e   g   a   p
s

left inherent
enabled
enter through the heart
exit wound the thought
to
out
of into

nothing

glimmers of holy goodbyes
effigies of hymns remembered
and faces forgotten
fractured
felt
followed

by   silence
shaking
slipping
slowing
slowing
slow
s
l
o
w-
 in

we must go on

go on,

on;

commemoration and amnesia

am i
an amnesiac
or a haemophiliac
or is this a heart attack?
that burns these holes in the lips
that shelters and stings
that blankets then burns
hurts and heals
to truth   to sadness
the   the
i devote
an increase in heartblood
to varnish and veneer
against their words that smear and snarl
i commemorate
i instigate
i must not fake
the this then why if how why and being
seeing feeling
crying of this silenced soul of tears and fears
that fall to stand
that fall to stand

how   i   remember
how   i   wish   to   forget

pathetic tosser wanker quimmo cripple cunt runt bender fucker
nothing nothing loser girl mammy's boy mammy's boy boy boy
BOY?

so i bottle your mind
with verbs that find
their place in nouns
of laced narcotic
underground
character disdenied
and undesigned and soul declined
i   bottle   your   mind
to commemorate
the pain this memory dawning
into   now
so know
so
no
and how i desecrate
to educate
and emancipate the chains that emaciate
the eyes that split my vision
the voices that stammered my tongue
yet now i speak
yet now i speak-
this war of attrition
this heartraged mission
this restricted code of breaking,   breaking   recognition
am i
an amnesiac
or a haemophiliac
or
is this
a heart   attack-

carelines

1.

the ghosts of you make the spirit in me
footsteps fade
but nature grows
through the chlorophyll
my darkness diminishes
within this water
your reflection flows
within these trees
your liferings lip
this is the place
where peace exists
this is the place
where mind resists
the temptation to force
through this place
fracture fuses
this is the place
where dirt is unsoiled
and time is the rustle of branches brattled and brown
the ghosts of you make the spirit in me
so go slow,inhabit the moment,
watch the meticulous melting ice upon frozenned blade
river flow mind grow
delicate minutes spent tasting nothing
but the sky above and the earth below
the spirit of me makes the ghosts of you
live.

2.

i stare at this mirror called man
it cuts my fingertips if i get too close
it magnifies memory
increases haemaglobin
in this breaking image of contemporary
ghosts linger
reflection triggers response
am i and i am
ringing in my head
stab my side and don't make a sound
slit my throat with your avarice
nail me to the cross
drown me in this vacuum
believe me if i say i'm sorry
deliver me from melancholia
castrate me if i tell you you're sexy
allow me some necrophillia
if i inhabit myself will i be guilty
of mirror gash and mind lack
drawn together by pulling back
corpse drawn synthesis of woman and man
let silence be my strength
let wound by my word

and so we move so we soothe

the memories that crack us

are the scars that make us-

3.

from wood stone and candle
you stand
a flame from fracture
in this silence
a wordlessened whisper
in this sadness
smile

such comfort in so culling this carrion
holding stitches from split
choked tears to tear thorax
you stand
a candle from cut
flowing light upon end   less   ened   night
covering flesh with feeling

again-

you stand
a poem worn by wound
strung out like bracelets
forming a forever from a never

again-

you are ourness organic
soul empathetic
a future fleshed from fear
a hand that is constantly near
like trees we grow needing light
like stones we know the silence of suicide night
like candles we see clear
we see clear.

again-

let being be

alone on a mountain
in
early spring
thinking of who and what i am
alone, amongst
soaked earth brittled trees
burntblack grass
and how i am to be a father to my children
in this severance
this sacrifice of soul
that spits solitude into every corner
and
here;
i fear i am an absent
a lostness concealed by wealth
i
i choke tears in supermarkets
hate people carriers
turn away from baby seats
buy crayons
tell the till operator my life story just to convince her i am a
parent
dream of tomorrow
but stay haunted by yesterday
and still
still these thoughts will not cease
they cascade like mountainpure water to some unknown yet
needed destination

these fragments i call mind
return
pecking at resilience
holing my hope
and here;
i swallow nature whole
trying to believe this must be it
there has to be a chance
a sky glint of somewhere starlight
that will burn holes into this darkness

and that the hands i made
will create me
that these fragments shall fuse a life
into fire
and that what i am
will let them be
who and what they wish to be

that all this pain this nocturnalled anxiety this waiting for
weekends to come and
that paul robeson robbie fowler the rock christina rossetti and
jackson pollock and a fragment of me
will somehow stay in their tinymassive minds

against this torrent called life we inhabit
and that somehow by going
i have never gone
only arrived at some cleaner point just like this water that rages
past me now
and that one day when they are men and women
that they may sit upon this mountain
under this sky
with calmed heart and
still
searching thoughts
and they may utter
the word
father
with some semblance
of beauty
and recognition
and

know

know
that
they
they
are
un-alone

forever.

Patrick Jones

Savage

Patrick Jones -
A Ranter for the 21st Century
by Phil Clark

I read the first draft of Patrick Jones' 'Everything Must Go' on the train between Paddington and Cardiff in 1997. The play had arrived on my desk unsolicited. I had no idea who Patrick Jones was - why should I? - he had never written a play before. By the time I had arrived in Cardiff and finished the script, I was exhausted, inspired and energised by what I had read. I was sure about one thing: I had to find out more about this unknown Jones, who was so passionate about finding a voice in 'these stammering times'.

It was the late '90s and Wales was at a crossroads in its life, with big changes on the horizon: the possibility of an Assembly looming, Welsh pop music making impressive statements in the cultural debate, and Welsh artists living and campaigning in the hope that the new Assembly would liberate and elevate the status of all working artists in Wales.

Into the midst of this came Patrick Jones: a new voice, but one rooted in the traditional socialism-for-change movement in Wales. In his poetry and his plays he displays a positive sense of outrage, and rare talent to say what he means and damn the consequences. The magazine *Plays International* said of his work in 1999 that his 'vision secures and reinvents the Welsh tradition of vivid imagery and a lyrical sense of poetry for a theatre of the new millennium.'

One of the most exciting features about Patrick's work is his determination that the arts in Wales can positively contribute to this 'stammering time'. Clearly he demostrates that if the National Assembly of Wales were to invest in its professional artists, the nation could emerge as a confident, determined and eloquent culture.

Jones has always been influenced by great public speakers who have gone before him. The tradition of orators such as John Bull, Gerard Winstanley, Abeizer Koppe, Aneurin Bevan and Tony Benn, who have been passionate about their politics in open public spaces and encouraged mass audiences towards political change, have inspired Jones to find a public arena for his words.

He is concerned with the power of language. Like his predecessors he demands a reaction; he challenges his audience to have an opinion and a response. Actors who have worked from his scripts talk about the joy of his language, and how it works better spoken out loud than on the page. With his poetry the same applies. He is of the same tradition as the performance poets of the '60s and '70s, who did much to popularise poetry and move it out of the singular domain of the middle class voice.

And it is the language that has a unique quality in Welsh theatre. In both English and Welsh we can observe an obsession for poetic language throughout the work of Welsh playwrights Dylan Thomas, Saunders Lewis, Gwyn Thomas, Sion Eirian and Ed Thomas. Patrick Jones is no exception. His writing fuses poetry and drama to develop this linguistic tradition and continues to make connections between drama, poetry and the song lyrics of Welsh pop bands.

Already his work has proven to be accessible and popular - two dangerous notions for Welsh art - and as usual, his packed playhouses, standing ovations and press recognition are not simply celebrated here in Wales, but rather viewed with envy, because, as The *Sheffield Telegraph* observed, 'This is not comfortable theatre. The language is blunt, the imagery stark and it is guaranteed to pierce even the toughest social conscience. And yet there is beauty in the way drama, poetry and music are combined.' That being said, there are those who will still ask - is it literature?

Jones' answer is simple: let's stop talking about, analysing and intellectualising. First let's do it, offer it to the people and let them be the judges. So far his approach seems to be working. There are no greater critics than the masses.

'Everything Must Go' is a revenge tragedy for the 1990s. Set in Blackwood, South Wales, five friends talk of their hopes and fears and the determination of their generation in pursuit of honesty and truth. They are the lost generation - 'a living exhibition of how not to be' - the generation without a voice - until now. Patrick Jones' stark drama puts the forgotten generation on stage. Premiered at the Sherman Theatre, Cardiff, in February 1999, Jones' first play attracted such an enormous amount of media attention that it demanded a National Tour and London residency in 2000. *The Guardian* said, "Everything Must Go' is striking enough to do for Welsh theatre what the Manics and Catatonia have done for its music - bring it to prominence as no longer a poor relation but the artistic equal of the rest of Britain.'

Although his work is dark, Jones is optimistic and often hopeful. The *Belfast Telegraph* wrote of 'Everything Must Go': 'This is a country with no industry to call its own, with massive unemployment, whose young people grow up believing that they can have everything, but are given none of the tools they need to lead their lives. Northern Ireland may have been bad, but at least there's a War to blame. Wales has been left on the slag heap and who's to blame for that?' Consequently, 'there is no denying the piece's power to speak to a young audience.' (*The Guardian*)

'Everything Must Go' was produced in association with the Manic Street Preachers and supported by a soundtrack which included the Manic Street Preachers, Stereophonics and Catatonia. The play is a fusion of music and theatre in which one art form serves to complement, enlighten and enrich the other. The result is an extraordinary piece of theatre which encompasses, and also challenges, all that has become known as 'Cool Cymru'. *The Independent* commented, 'Jones' first play drinks deeply from the well of assonance and ancient traditions of Welsh lyricism.'

Whilst 'Everything Must Go' is a very Welsh play, it is essentially a collage of modern Britain at the time of the millennium. The themes it explores, such as unemployment, industrialisation, disenchantment with New Labour and drug abuse, are issues that remain universal to communities across Britain. The *Daily Telegraph* observed that it '... voices the feelings of a whole generation', and The *Western Mail* commented that it was 'a thrilling moment of Welsh theatre'.

Patrick Jones' second play, 'Unprotected Sex', again commissioned and presented by the Sherman Theatre in 1999, includes many of the themes of 'Everything Must Go', but is a play that begins to examine maleness. 'It is a brave and powerful exploration of the harm caused by the emotional repression inherent in traditional male culture.' (*The Independent*)

The play is, again, set in the South Wales Valleys, and centres around Gary, a deserter from the Kosovo conflict who still insists on wearing his army kit. He has witnessed the atrocities of Kosovo and, although a deserter, cannot escape the exploding bombs and images in his mind. But there is a limit to his girlfriend's tolerance. Upstairs their neighbour, Denver, has been bullied by Gary as a child and, seeking refuge amongst the mountain ponies, has witnessed his own atrocities - the mindless murder of a pregnant mare. 'Unprotected Sex' is a play which demands reaction from the audience; often brutal, Jones explores relationships and the sheer torrent of words is irresistible. 'A chamber piece of pain,' declared *The Independent*.

You can read Patrick Jones' plays, you can read his poems, you can listen to his cd performance poetry 'Commemoration and Amnesia', but there is no greater night out than watching him perform his poetry live on stage. He stamps his foot, he rants his poetry, he rips his books, he burns flags. You just never know what he'll do next. See and hear him live - you won't forget his words.

This book records the work of someone at the beginning of his career. His achievements during these three years have been remarkable. When you meet Patrick, he is shy and often uncomfortable with the world, but inside him is a torrent of emotion and words that explode upon the page as he writes. He writes for tomorrow, but is indebted to the past. He struggles, he rants - he is a ranter for the 21st century.

Phil Clark

2001

emg: oliver ryan & maria pride
photograph jane linz roberts

everything must go

first performed in February 1999 at
The Sherman Theatre in Cardiff

director: Phil Clark
designer: Jane Linz Roberts
lighting designer: Ceri James

cast
a: Oliver Ryan
pip: Roger Evans
cindy: Maria Pride
jim: Andrew Lennon
curtis: Rhys Miles Thomas
worthington: Brendan Charleson

emg: oliver ryan & roger evans

photograph jane linz roberts

everything must go

ACT 1

UNIT 1

Voices through a loudspeaker:

A:	Oh land of my fathers so dear to me
CURTIS:	famed land of the minstrel
CINDY:	the home of the free
PIP:	thy warriors who wielded undaunted thy sword
	for freedom their lifeblood hath poured
JIM:	thy rocks and thy crags o'er thy valleys keep guard
A:	thy mountains still shelter the haunts of the bard
PIP:	thy rills
CINDY:	and thy brooks
CURTIS:	sing their way to the sea
A:	in music so moving to me
JIM:	though foremen have trampled in triumph thy vales
A:	yet fail they to silence the old tongue of wales
CURTIS:	thy harpstrings unbroken by traitor's fell hand
ALL:	Still sing to me songs of my land
ALL:	Still sing to me songs of my land
PIP:	There aint no commitments round yer.....

UNIT 2

MUSIC: 'A design for life'
[MANIC STREET PREACHERS]

During the music the cast stand and face the audience, faces tight,
taut, cold and lost; they begin to act out typical teenage acts,
exaggeratedly - one smokes; one drinks; another injects a needle; one
writes a poem; another slits her wrists; another cuts her chest;
another screams; one watches the audience; another cradles a baby;
a couple make love; a couple argue. The music stops and they face
the audience and pray.

UNIT 3

NARRATOR:

See, we didn't start this you know, we we we didn't
start this fucking war we call living today ok ok we
we didn't start it we we jus grew up amongst it all,
didn't have a choice really did we say did we?
Thought you sorted it out after the war didn't you,
say, didn't the fuck you? Fucking e-rad-i-cate
fucking WANT fucking DISEASE bastard
IGNORANCE fucking SQUALOR and
IDLENESS say didn't you - sort the working class
out you said - well take a fucking look take a
fucking look around you.
We are the generation with no name the x y z e
generation go on go on label us go on go on - we
are the them the the them the losing the don't care

know nothing have everything generation we are
the frightened generation the the anything
generation come - come on down come on down -
welcome welcome to the pain welcome to the
beauty welcome to YOUR monster 2000 welcome
to the piss stained rain cleansed bus stops and crack
alleys of wales today your wales your fucking wales -
go on go on - come on come on down your lovely
(fake welsh accent) wales - lovely innit - oh aye -
lovely - how green is my valley how grey is the sky -
oooh lovely love - fucking daffodils dancing in the
spring sun - fucking new deal employers fucking
leeks and rugged scrum halves up to their bollocks
in mud shouting numbers in the rain - the pubs
puking souls out out out on saturday nights - the
the the fucking joyriders burning the hillsides - the
temazes stuck on tongues - the sulphur glow of
orange lamps - the sound of factories at dawn - the
karaoke queens in cymmer - green hills - choirs -
male of course - come on taste it feel it come on
down - lissen to this choir - cunts - lissen -
Welcome to your fears welcome to your dreams
welcome to the welsh tourist board's translation
clinic - welcome to the real nuts and fucking bolts
welcome to the burning eyes the torn torsos the
gaping wounds - the - history - pistory - piss story -
welcome welcome - to the psychiatric hospital we
we all live in - welcome welcome - bore-fucking-da
-

MUSIC: 'Masses against the classes'
[MANIC STREET PREACHERS]

UNIT 4

Broken down playground. Dark lonely hum of the valleys. Swings and slides. Five youngsters in their early 20's loll around spitting, kicking and talking. The sound of a factory hooter in the distance.

PIP: See that merc Johnny nicked yesterday, tonned it up Tredegar he did, coppers couldn't catch im he said, good laugh ol Johnny good piss taker - i wouldn't mind getting one myself tonight - saw some smart bmws down chartists view, rich wankers wouldn't miss em if i did anyway - standing there with their posh alarms and crook locks - bollocks - simple as fuck -

JIM: i used to know this bloke right, who was the first person to break into a fucking mondeo right, first person - ever like - *(astonished by the fact)*

CINDY: big fucking deal - why -

PIP: how did he do it en?

JIM: don't know he wouldn't tell me-

CINDY: what's this thing bout cars en say, for fucks sake?

PIP: aw cum on mun Cind it's fuckin' brilliant mun, the speed the buzz, better'n'sex -

CINDY: i bet it is with you - why are you always going on about cars, cars an drinking cars an nicking, cars an coppers, speed and sex - an look at you you couldnt run ten yards without collapsing in a fucking heap - cars cars cars - know wha' they say -

PIP: bout wha' -

JIM: whassa en -

CINDY: about men an cars?

PIP:	*(seemingly interested)* nah, what do they say?
CINDY:	they say tha' a man that always goes on bout cars an stuff - got a small dick!
PIP:	bollocks, that's a load of bollocks - wha' - read tha' in one of your feminist mags eh cind?
JIM:	fuck off mun Cind - jus' fuck off - i don't even like cars ok, ok like?
CINDY:	ok ok nipple dicks what car are you gonna nick today then - *(sarcastically)* rolls royce?
PIP:	shut up -
CINDY:	it's jus' boring - you going on about cars all the time - can't even drive.
PIP:	thas not the point - point is to beat the biz - beat 'em at it like - nick the car - give the coppers a good chase like then ditch it or torch the fucker on the mountain and fuck off back to bed like - anyways i can drive - wanna cum for a spin?
CINDY:	fuck off -
PIP:	what's the matter wiv you - time of the month eh? - how many girls wiv their period does it take to change a lightbulb - 4 right - why'sa'en? *(shouts)* it jus' does ok it jus' fuckin' does!!
JIM:	why'sa'en - i - i don't get it mun -
CINDY:	fuck off willya bernard manning - if someone said it was their menstrual cycle you'd try an nick it -
PIP:	wha - talking fucking femmi again eh cind?
JIM:	i 'ad a chopper once - red one - fucking lovely it was....
A:	come on you pair - give it a rest mun
PIP:	oh, it speaks - it fucking speaks - whasamatta wiv you mun haven't said a word about nothing eh -
JIM:	it's anything
PIP:	what -

JIM: you haven't said a word about anything

PIP: what -

JIM: can't have two negatives ina fuckin' sentence -

All look astonished at JIM

PIP: right ok butt, sorry about tha' - fuck me

A: just a bit quiet tha's all - you wouldn't understand - can you see that star up there....can you....*(points up to the sky)*

CURTIS: *(who has remained quiet throughout)* staring at the world you'll never change

PIP: oh, very fucking funny, who said tha' anyway, fucking ghandhi eh curtis - why do you always talk in fucking riddles mun - haven't got a clue what you're on about - speak fucking english like the rest of us mun - fuck's sake -

CURTIS: yeah and use fuck in every other sentence - no thanks - an anyway - nothing wrong with quotes - say more than most people - it was Therapy and the song is Nowhere - good title innit?

PIP: *(seriously)* say, know any more about cars like - i could spray paint them on the fuckers 'en couldn't i?

CURTIS: drive away and it's the same -

A: yeah, tha's true nothing changes nothing ever changes roun yer nothing it's all grey fucking grey and rainy - shitty little houses satellite dishes an pubs -

A: this is my truth now tell me yours

CINDY: who said tha' 'en?

PIP: fuck me give it a rest will you - what you ever gonna do bout anything say - fuck all

A: aneurin bevan did -

JIM: who cares

A: he fucking did

CURTIS: if you tolerate this then your children will be next -

JIM: no - you will fucking be -

CINDY: i wanna score mun

A: always the answer innit cind

CURTIS: drive away an it's the same -

CINDY: can't keep lissening to all this babble mun - i'm off boys - leave you to your sega - *(Cindy exits in search of a fix)*

CURTIS: come on everybody come together try love one another -

A: i'm reading this really good book about -

PIP: what the fuck do you know - jus' come back from yankeeland wiv your ideas and fucking bollocks about bastard alienation of the worker - seen the fucking new deal mate - tried working for one of those japcunt factories cos there's nowt else to do - say - fuck your books live in the real world mun - remember where you came from - right -

A: lissen pip alright - i do - right - i know where i came from and i know what i came back to - yer - righting fucking yer - yeah, right - i went away cos i couldn't stick it yer no long -

JIM: any longer

PIP: fuck up mun

A: so i ran from these sad streets of satellite suns that stare - ran off to america lost myself in chicago snow and neon glow but then what? i was lonely there it wasn't the american dream at all it was fucking lonely and fucking sad - so i thought - fuck

	it i'm coming home - so i came back and i i i tried to believe in this place - fucking chartists meeting in rain soaked caves up in fucking Cwm and Brynmawr,
CURTIS:	We are the only ones left to believe in
A:	fucking Aneurin Bevan uppona hill speaking to fucking thousands of people bout life an stuff jus' like my dad used to tell me an my brother when we wuz younger
PIP:	get the fuck on wiv it will ya - wanker - i gotta shit - aye - so you came back saw how great it is and decided to stay - finished now - can i go for a shit now then can i?
CURTIS:	can you still remember say where is the tomorrow
A:	no, not really, i've just fucking begun
PIP:	well - iyave, i'm fucking bursting mun - what more is there to say -
JIM:	you should be on jerry fucking springer mun - wha's 'appened to you mun a?
PIP:	it's great place to live mun- got my own job flat shag fucking kenwood holidays inna summer what more is there lads? *(gets wallet out)* look at all these mun - I can do what the fuck i want - look mun - look at all these - *(shows cards)*
JIM:	fucking ALDI clubcards you daft cunt
CURTIS:	and in these plagued streets of pity we can buy anything ...
PIP:	*(more thoughtfully)* look- we're all fucking losers all fucking stuck yer in some cunting prison or other it's jus' tha' i get on wiv it- i know i'm gonna fucking live an die yer - i know that ok - but fuck you wiv your middle class bollocks an stuff - you can't understand me - or wha' i feel - you don't

	know why i nick cars a book can't tell you tha' - i earned my poverty ok-
CURTIS:	motown junk a lifetime of slavery - motown junk
A:	i don't say i do - i said i hadda come back like
JIM:	i yerd some twat on about his therapist yesterday - fucking cunt of a suit he was - no style and didn't have a clue about jung -
PIP:	you really surprise me sometimes you really do -
JIM:	*(feeling proud of himself)* thanks it's jus' cos some cunt gotta suit on he thinks he's got it all - when really he hasn't got a fucking clue - i had the cunt's wallet anyway - give the money to old joe down by the library - there - that's fucking socialism for you A?
A:	yeah fucking right Jim - nice one......
JIM:	i just got fuck all to do so i watch the open university at night

Curtis, A and Pip all look at Jim in total disbelief but a moment of peace and friendship exists on stage

A:	all gone wrong yer mun all fucking wrong fuck me - stick whole tribes up on mountains and call it choice - fucking spar's the staple diet of whole fucking communities and i i i thought we'd be better off under labour but fuck bmw - we got fucking freedom - oh fuck me - i jus' remembered i got one of those fucking new deal interviews tomorrow at a bastard electrical shop oh fuck what if i get the fucker?
A:	you'll be alright Jim - i'm sure -

CINDY reappears looking high, tousled and confident

CURTIS: i look to the sky it makes me cry
CINDY: oh Curt don't worry, relax mun - pip give it a rest
            mun?
PIP: nah, i'm sick of lissening to him mun - accept it we
            are all losers ok - ok?
A: go on fuck off - you'll see one you fucking will -
PIP: bollocks mate i'm off - leave you lot in the rain -
            coming Curt coming jim?

CURTIS, Jim and PIP walk offstage.

CINDY: A- why why why are you so angry, so ready to
            destroy mun, why why - i mean he's a prat an all
            but Pip's got a point - why are you so fucking
            angry?
A: it's just something i carn work out like - too
            painfilled like -
CINDY: like wha' - what do you mean?
A: he - like - well - he like - um - well there's a lot of
            fucking things that get me angry for fuck's sake love
            - and you know that i nor you can do a fucking
            thing about them - here like - fucking lost-in these
            rain pelted streets of pity we are fucking lost - yer
            home is where the pain is-
CINDY: there you go again, calm down please mun A calm
            down you're ranting your eyes bulging your words i
            can't take it much longer, i fucking can't mun (*goes
            to get something from inside her jacket*)
A: leave it Cind - i thought you'd stopped -
CINDY: fuck up then -
A: look Cind there's too many bodybags too many
            police conferences too many adverts too much

choice too many bullets too much too much - right
- sorry - right - my dad right - well - see it was like -
but - fucking hell - like my dad well this company
that he'd worked for for 10 years after the pit closed
- one of those faceless fucking factories on one of
those ever so beautiful industrial estates - so - he
has to work for them like 9 hours a day packing
TVs and videos in cardboard boxes stood there in
the cold one day with one little window to look out
of - asking when to go for a piss having to walk a
fucking line so he don't waste any time getting
there and then timed when he is in there - so, he
worked there, never missed a day, never - hated it
yeah but believed in supporting his family like - take
a look Blair you fucker - take a look - so he battled
on packing those cunting little boxes day after day
week after week life after life - never could afford
one though - marx was right - sorry - sorry - so just
before Christmas he goes in as normal, fucking
uniform all ironed as usual and when he goes to
pick up his clocking in card it's gone like, so he
goes up to the office feeling like a fucking
schoolboy an asks for it and they tell him to go to
another office and then the manager so he goes up
there and Worthington, the fucking human
resources manager of the shit hole, tells him he is
no longer needed - that he has become surplus to
requirement and his cards are downstairs in the
office - goodbye - good fucking bye mate - no sorry
no handshake no rights no nothing nothing
nothing - fuck - it destroyed my dad - kicked him
right down - he jus' stood there and said nothing
when he really wanted to scream and shout and hit

the cunt but instead bottled it up all inside and didn't say a fucking word - so he walked out of that fucking plaastic watercoloured pastel office downa steps past the line and nobody, not a fucking dead soul of them looked up or said a fucking word
- as if nothing, nothing had happened - jus' carried on as normal -

CINDY: sorry, i'm sorry A i really fucking am, i know, it's not fucking fair it happens all the time i know i yerd about -

A: look cind, it happened to my dad - to my fucking dad - who'd put food on our table and given every fucking penny he'd ever earned to help us, clothes, shoes, trips, every fucking thing fuck he hardly ever spent anything on himself and then - SMASH - gone - thank you and goodnight - gone

CIND: see - i need another fucking hit

A: fucking leave it mun Cind will you - so he jus' sat in our kitchen reading the dictionary - said he wanted to enrich his vocabulary and he went so fucking quiet - lost interest in everything and i would look over at him and see his mind burning the fuck up like - but he couldn't speak about it like - fuck - i've seen him out in the snow and frost in january down on his hands and knees planting seeds into the ground - said something must grow something must grow - fingers bleeding scraping the ground trying to get those fucking things into the ground - something must grow - god - fucking hell mun - see Cind can't you see it didn't have to happen and i hate tha' bastard Worthington and i hate those Korean cunts for carrying on in their shit little world using us like bastard fodder - i - i can't let it

go on i gotta take a stand - do something like -
fucking hell - this bastard place mun - we are all on
our knees fucking grovelling to the cunts in suits -
no choice too much choice - we should - rid this
country of fuckers like him - wipe the scum off from
the earth -

CINDY: i know i know but who the fuck decides who's
scum i know you know but who can decide - look A
i got so much fucking anger and pain inside me but
i've never hit anyone in my life can't face it makes
things worse - so i i -

A: i know - cut yourself - that's not going to sort
anything out is it mun Cind fuck me i've bandaged
you up more than a fucking mummy mun - and still
the cunts kill - see!!!

CINDY: not as easy as tha' A - ok - it helps me face this
(points all around) it's all about pain control -

A: well i'll do it my way alright - no one no one should
have to work in those fucking factories like fucking
living death camps -

CINDY: can, can we talk about something else - please?

A: thanks for lissening Cind - i'm off to talk to dad
about things ok - don't worry - i'll be ok - alright -
thanks -

CINDY: A - be fucking careful ok?

A: ok - ta see you later - Cind -

*(A walks off into the night - Cindy retrieves a bleach bottle from her
bag and pours it all over the seats, slide, swings and floor and
furiously cleans up, then takes out a razor blade, rolls up her sleeve
and cuts her forearm - and looks up to the sky -)*

CINDY: god - you bastard - why did you create such a

beautiful place - and then leave it to humans - why?
Something must grow, something must grow

(The blood drips onto the ground)

UNIT 5

The interior of a factory, cold clinical and neat. 14 machines worked mostly by young men and women dressed in white uniforms except one man of about 55. They are robotically inserting something metal into videos and then putting them onto a conveyor belt. From his office at the side of the factory space Worthington enters the shop floor with a clipboard and is checking that everyone is well turned out and wearing their name badges. He is the Human Resources Manager. A factory hooter blasts.

UNIT 6

MUSIC: 'Motorcycle emptiness'
[MANIC STREET PREACHERS]

(Enter person. The word WANT is spray painted onto the back wall.)

NARRATOR:

see - take a look around you, look carefully see - we - we we we are a bit confused - unsure of things too many choices not enough jobs too many jobs not enough choices - too many things to want that we really don't know what we need - unsure generation, spoilt, you may say can't we have it all the sign says it could be you it could be you - we can have it all now can't we just like the adverts say just like the adverts - what. what do we need? what do WE want? so many fads so many drugs i don't know if my arse is talking the same thing as my mouth - so. so many ways to die today - so many - so many - haagen dazs and cocaine - make me real - make me feel.

But still we are not happy you say - you say - it wasn't like this when you was a lad you say. say. say - so what are we to do then eh Mr fucking Careers Advisor what are we gonna do en? what do we fucking WANT? what do i want then say what do i want - i want it fucking all ok - i want it all - need a car carn afford one nick one - need some money carn get any - do some thieving get sum - wan' sum blow do a deal nick a car get sum - it's a vicious fucking circle mun - carn get offait - so give me my credit card my amex fun my orange visa vodafone my scratch card my speed my e my my my fucking nothing - fuck, my ead is exploding - cook it whizz it shove it up my arse - forget it all in a fucking instant - forget forget forget fucking IT!! want want want - taste it fuck it eat it shit it smell it fake it take it - cuts my tongue and slits my wrists if i think too hard - you can her and her and him - you can buy anything - daz ultra virgin scoot goldfish goldfish? goldfish - fucking marbles I NEED FUCKING MARBLES ... what next eh - eh - eh - so many ways to kill yourself - dances diseases, drugs, days, nights, night so wha' do i want 'en - what do i fucking want? give me a needle a basement bed a nicotine tongue kiss give me give me - more and more hits rushes fixes ways to fill the fucking holes -

holes holes - oh give me what i want - give
me.......... death....... *(slower)* give me nothing -
please oh please give me what i want - give me
death - give me peace - please please - please

UNIT 7

MUSIC: 'Ready for drowning'
[MANIC STREET PREACHERS]

7 miners climb out of the ground and sit in lecture chairs, brought
on by factory workers, and are presented with computer screens.
After failing to work out how to use them, each miner picks up his
screen and throws it down into the pit. They take a long look at the
audience, their lamps shining straight out, then exit.

A factory hooter sounds. Silence.

UNIT 8

CINDY and A are all alone at the park. It is quiet, night.

A: I've been thinking....
CINDY: Do you know i really hate this place - our home - i
     really do - everything has changed everything is so
     fucking different now - i don't know what to feel
     anymore - when i was young, everything seemed so
     beautiful so so so in its place, so real and natural
     like even the rain didn't seem so dark and desperate
     - fields skies grass trees swifts and stars just life
     everywhere - it's like today right - fucking St.

David's day like and i was watching all the little kids
dressed up like welshgirls and rugby players an ah -
with their innocent eyes so happy to be doing
summat different and exciting - all dreesed up in
red so fiery warm and free - all those daffodils leeks
words and stories - then they step out into all this -
doesn't make fucking sense does it? where the fuck
ave we gone wrong mun?

A: i know Cind - i fucking know -

CINDY: ever felt like killing yourself?

A: sumtimes but then i think - fuck it i won't let the
cunts beat me tha' easy and i sort of pull out of it-

CINDY: sumtimes i feel like splitting myself right open down
the middle and letting everything bleed out of me -

A: fuck me mun Cind - hold on mun-

CINDY: no lissen - letting everything bleed out of me out
out onto the mountain or summat and into the
ground - like a new start or summat - something
must grow, something must grow - start again like -

A: i wish you wouldn't do tha' - honest mun - i've
been thinking how i'm gonna get Worthington -
think i'll pretend i'm applying for a job then get 'im
all to myself in his office-and get the fucker - or
maybe i'll trap 'im down on the shop floor an make
'im make fucking crap videos all day - then kill the
cunt -

CINDY: still on about tha' en?

A: yeah, gotta cind, fucking gotta

CINDY: well ok up to you - anyway i was talking about how
much i hate it yer - no purpose like -

A: stop killing yourself with fucking chemicals and shit
- what is the point -

CINDY: it makes life seem bearable - it's a way of coping -

A: so pour sum shit into your veins then slash it out
            isit? Is tha' what happened with you and Curt eh -

CINDY: i don't wanna talk about tha' - at least i'm not
            hurting anyone am i? do you wanna feel when you
            look around - blind me with tears cover my eyes -
            slice my ear off i don't wanna hear no more -

A: why not cut sum other fucker mun Cind -

CINDY: my scars remind me that i'm alive -

A: drugs are no answer

CINDY: drugs destroy them them them -

A: yeah - but we gotta do something be someone -
            they won't fucking beat me Cind, they won't - i'll
            kill Worthington and i'll go on and on and on - i
            will - i believe in my mind in my thoughts and they
            can never take that away from me -

CINDY: you've - got - to - feel - nothing. nothing. it is the
            only way A - FUCK. GOD? NOTHING. DRUGS.
            SCARS. i love them i hate them i feel safe i feel
            shattered in them like no-one no-one can touch me
            - all orange and red like - it's all too fucking fragile
            mun - we could break at any moment - we're all
            fucked -

A: no, Cindy - we are not - gotta do sumthing fight
            fight fight back - we will win in the end - by
            refusing to lose we have already won -

CINDY: win what?

A: life

CINDY: death

A: life

CINDY: but i still don't know wha' to do - where to go - the
            buses only go to Cardiff and smell of piss an smoke
            there ain't no sun - no sun - nothing can grow here

	- nothing can - *(starts to cry)*
A:	it's grey forever unless we make it green make it green -
CINDY:	Listen ... do you know I used to look out of my bedroom window and see this field, this beautiful field full of daffodils and every spring there'd be this massive glow and i'd know it'd soon be getting warmer and the birds soon be singing and I just felt I belonged..
A:	I know
CINDY:	but then one day - I woke up and heard the sound of diggers and bulldozers and wham - they'd wrecked my field ripped it up to build a fucking car park *(gets knife out)* ... see
A:	Cind
CINDY:	it was then that I started cutting...my friend my safety my belonging

UNIT 9

PIP, CURTIS and JIM are breaking into a shop with a metal shutter in front of it.

PIP:	all clear is it -
CURTIS:	yeah
JIM:	yeah, yeah come the fuck on will you - quick -
PIP:	ok ok i'm doing my fucking best mun - not easy they change the locks every fucking week -
CURTIS:	this wonderful world of purchase power -
PIP:	shut it Curt for fuck's sake - wha' do you wan'?
JIM:	wouldn't mind some batteries - fucking herd of the

	cunts for my remote control car - fucking uses 'em like fuck
PIP:	jim - fuck up mun - this is serious - how bout a ghetto blaster for tonite uppa stones ?
JIM:	sounds good major Pip - *(studies the shutter closely)* look boys it says yer... CAR TRAP BEHIND SHUTTERS - oh yeah, i'm really gonna stop and read that as i'm ramming the cunt eni-
CURTIS:	only takes one match-
PIP:	bastard rip off innit - fucking Robin Hood we are -
JIM:	wish i 'ad a bottle -
PIP:	me too - fuck me you've started now - come on you sad bastard -
CURTIS:	to wear the scars to SHOW where i came from -
JIM:	i'll jus' twat this 'larm and we'll be in -

Burglar alarm sounds, they all jump, scared-

PIP:	Jim - Jim
JIM:	wha -
PIP:	do you know, breaking innna shop is a bit like shagging an ugly girl -
JIM:	whys'a'en?
PIP:	you want to have to but are a little bit scared so you close your eyes and once you're in it feels great -
JIM:	*(ponders the image for a while)* yeah- guess you're right - i've only shagged ugly girls so i wouldn't know the fucking difference like -
CURTIS:	the green green grass of home -
BOTH:	Tom fucking Jones - know tha' one Curt - nice one -
PIP:	like i said get some stuff then uppa stones have a laugh - oh fuck life is alright sumtimes anit?

JIM: i always feel as if i've beat the fucking system after
            i've nicked a car or done a shop -
PIP: you've never nicked a car -
CURTIS: first time i did it for the hell of it -
JIM: i fucking did coppers caught me -
PIP: you broke in and then fucking fell asleep mun -
            look out Ronnie fucking Biggs -
JIM: anyfuckingway i was saying like - i feel like i am in
            control and that the fuckers carn get to me - Pip -
PIP: wha -
JIM: be nice one day to have a nice fucking girlfriend
            with a car and an 'ouse wouldn't it - do you think
            like ah sometimes - settle down and mow the lawn
            on sundays wash the car and sleep after a big nosh -
            aye and you can have a shag anytime you want too -
PIP: fuck me mun - you are mad - wha' you on mun -

*They manage to open the lock and burst in - we don't see them in the
shop - and they emerge clutching a ghetto blaster and Jim with
hundreds of packs of batteries.*

JIM: aw fuck wha' am i gonna do now - bastards
PIP: pick the fuckers up before the cops cum mun- what
            do you fancy tonight uppa stone - temazes of coke
            say - how much you got?
JIM: 15 pence
CURTIS: sell my body on the street -
PIP: 15 fucking pence - carn do nothing with tha' -
JIM: carn do anything -
PIP: fuck up mun - whatever carn even have a piss for
            tha' -
JIM: i knew this kid right who - like - 'ad two fucking
            batteries in'is car - one for the car and one for his

	fucking fuck off stereo and when i asked him why he said - "because the bigger the stereo the more girls will talk to you and the better chance you got at 'aving a shag"- fucking 'ell like - kids today -
CURTIS:	i smell that smell it's that time of year again -
PIP:	look lads we've got fucking power-freedom aven't we - the cunts carn touch us -
JIM:	nah - fucking right Pip mind you i gotta go for tha' bastard new deal interview tomorrow - fuckin' wank tha' is - they got me bya short'n'curlies - fuckers -
PIP:	don't worry Jim i'll ramraid the fucking place for you- where is it?
JIM:	i think it's yer -

PIP and CURTIS look amazed

PIP:	why didn't you tell us then - your prints'll be all over the fucking place -
JIM:	*(Feeling proud of himself)* carn offer me the fucking job then can they -
PIP:	nice one nice one -
CURTIS:	in the beginning when we were winning -
JIM and PIP:	
	come on Curt coming uppa stones -
CURTIS:	My actions make me beautiful they dignify the flesh

UNIT 10

MUSIC:'Mountains'
[James Dean Bradfield]

NARRATOR:

The word IGNORANCE is spray painted on the
back wall
- so - who's responsible - whose mess is this - point
the finger press the button electrify the current
burn the book eh eh who is to blame? shoot the
young generation - make them bleed jus' as they
cause bleeding - what about the bible - koran -
national ssservice - the birch - bring back hanging -
let them have it - have it; what about the rich fat
bastards who make all the decisions all the rights
and wrongs who starts the wars who sells the drugs
who burns the crosses who jacks off to internetted
it all starts somewhere - it'll all end nowhere -
education is not just something we did at school -
violence exists we did not stab first - hate is
apparent we did not hate first - don't think we
don't know who is guilty - we may seem apathetic
hate too much care too little don't appreciate
anything lost and arrogant to you - yeah - this is
true - we are so far apart cut adrift in an ocean of
needles morphine and vodka but prozac ain't no
bandage to this much blood - *(we see the factory
workers dressed in white at their machines;
Worthington walks down the line checking their
names off against a list on his clipboard)* can't you
see you've created this us i me you us created this
fucking fracture of history - arbeit macht frei - work
makes you free - we are covered in your blood - we
came we saw - we died
- we we are your critical mirror - look and look
deep - we know you know we know -

factory siren

UNIT 11

The playground. PIP, CURTIS and JIM shamble up to CINDY and A.

PIP:	what you two hanging around yer for - better be careful - you'll get arrested you will -
JIM:	i got a fucking 'uge pile of batteries -
CINDY:	for your vibrator eh Jim -
JIM:	whassaen?
PIP:	nevermind - you two coming uppa stones?
CURTIS:	if you don't want me to destroy you -
CINDY:	nah - fuck all to do mun -
A:	i'm going to kill Worthington - kill him - i've decided -
PIP:	what the fuck are you on mun - fuck it gets worse - been on the mushrooms again? -
CINDY:	he told me today - he won't lissen mun - let him - what's the point of trying to stop him - he's decided -
PIP:	aw cum on mun -
CURTIS:	to wear the scars -
PIP:	shut it right
CURTIS:	to show from where i came from
JIM:	where i came from -
PIP:	fuck up the pair of you -
A:	mr peter Worthington personnel manager of Kobashio tv and video of Afan Taff road Blackwood South bastard Wales UcuntingK the fucking world -
JIM:	got a postcode for tha' eh A - fuck me mun -
PIP:	who is he anyway - why the fuck are you going to

kill him? -

CINDY: he sacked his dad -

CURTIS: walk in silence

PIP: wha - he sacked your dad so now in your supreme
           wisdom you're gonna kill him - oh well that's ok
           then - go on go right fucking on - you're madder
           than i thought -

A: well, i've got my reasons and i'm just sick of things
           and gotta do something -

PIP: oh come on it happens all the fucking time - i hate
           most bastards more than you A but fuck me i'm not
           going to go and kill the cunts am i - it's its
           "economics"- in the "current economic climate" we
           must expect such "human shedding in the
           workplace" especially in the "service sectors" -
           don't be a prat - adapt and survive - ok wanker -
           now don't be a fool - come an ave a popper -

*CINDY paces around looking agitated and burning playing with
a razor blade in her pocket - she accidentally cuts herself-*

CINDY: ah - fuck it -

PIP: whassamatta Cind - carn stick a pace -

CINDY: how many men does it take to change a lightbulb?
           none right - cos they're all comparing cocks -

A: lissen right Pip - you fucking get me down right -
           fuckin couldn't give a toss can you - until it's your
           fucking turn - always got the gob aven't you -
           human shedding economics - fucking hell you
           don't even know wha' it means - this is fucking
           people - this is my fucking dad

PIP: shurrup - you're gonna kill some dickhead who's
           ruled by the japcunts - fucking revolution man -

CURTIS: all of our sins are attempts to fill the voids -

A: i'm not arguing with you ok - i'm gonna kill him -
              so fuck your *(shouts)* - economics your human
              shedding your workplace redundancy - he's got it
              coming an it's as simple as ah - right?

CINDY: calm down love - calm down mun -

PIP: *(sarcastically)* calm down calm down - shut the fuck
              up - leave 'im we all take fucking falls -

CURTIS: they dress your cage in its nature

A: i'll be ok jus' leave me alone - i i i i've gotta go an
              talk to dad *(runs off into the night)*

CINDY: why did you do tha' mun - you know how he is

PIP: ah - jus' winding him up - he gets on my tits with
              his preaching and do tha' do this crap - it 'appens
              all the time mun - no need to go an kill someone is
              there now? he won't do it anyway - probably read
              about it in some book - you coming uppa stones we
              gonna shoot some billy - up for it?

CINDY: nah too cold

CURTIS: the harder i try to learn something from you -
              further away - further away -

CINDY: - well - i'll see - maybe - i'll see what i've got to
              wear -

PIP: whooh!! - why does he wear tha' stuff roun his eyes
              for - say -

CURTIS: we are not your sinners our voices are for real

CINDY: you know Pip - bout school anallah - makes him see
              better he says -

PIP: yeah, that right eh - well hope he'll be able to see
              tha' bloke Worthington alright - you coming as well
              Ghandhi - why all the fucking riddles mun -

CURTIS: words words words to whip frighten - it's education
              no obligation - for emancipation - all we got

	sometimes -
CINDY:	forever and ever *(looks gently at CURTIS who goes shy and awkward)*
PIP:	don't start now you two - look i know you think i'm fucking thick or summat jus' because i don't agree wiv your ideas an stuff - it's jus' i can't ok ok -
CURTIS:	seemed so easy to not go too far -
CINDY:	but Pip you are always too hard on A you know he's lie tha' mun - deep down he's like you really -
PIP:	oh yeah - he's always going on about the revolution and stuff like tha' mun - meet the new boss same as the old one like - oh fuck me i'm getting as bad as you fucking pair now -
CURTIS:	it only takes one match to burn a thousand trees - only -
PIP:	let me finish will you - ok - i may smoke some H have a pint nick a car do a deal fuck a copper over but i got a fucking heart mun - i do know right from wrong - ok - ofuckingk?
CURTIS:	you stole the sun from my heart -
CINDY:	i know - i mean Pip - one day p'raps you'll get on wiv A an stuff -
CURTIS:	but i love you all the same -
CINDY:	*(stops still as he says the words)* - gotta do - gotta do something
PIP:	an killing some old fucker inna factory is gonna solve the problem isit?
CINDY:	i know i know -
CURTIS:	love carn fix the holes they made -
JIM:	What's happening Pip?

UNIT 12

MUSIC: 'International Velvet'
[CATATONIA; a version sung by children]

11 Welsh women enter, playing various children's games - it is early evening. One girl is excluded from all the games and she cradles a Welsh doll.
As they exit, the last girl drops the doll and Cindy runs to pick it up.

CINDY: you are so beautiful so fucking beautiful so pure so
           untouched by the them you are a picture my love, a
           picture that i'll hold forever - they didn't
           understand - they didn't understand - you do
           though don't you my love, you do - my love -

CINDY takes a razor blade out and slashes her forearm and bleeds onto the doll

CINDY: There my love, there - we are joined we are one - all
           clean and beautiful all clean and beautiful - you will
           grow you will grow -

UNIT 13

MUSIC: 'A Thousand Trees'
[STEREOPHONICS]

A is at the Aneurin Bevan Stones - four immense stones beneath a starry sky. He starts a soliloquoy:

A: it's so quiet now so deathly quiet i can just hear the
thrum of the road taking people away, away - and
see the orange glow of the factory lights far off on
the hill, so quiet now Nye so fucking quiet - what
would you think now eh? fucking new labour old
tories - bunch of fucking tossers all of them - even
the Welsh ones for fuck's sake - all they been
concerned about is unbanning beef on the
fuckingbone don't worry about the nhs falling apart
and perfectly healthy kidneys being removed as long
as you can have your beef bollocks - see - i didn't
know much about you - never taught it in fucking
school, all bastard Churchill - but my dad told me
about you and how you lived just up from us and
what you did for us like - and i remember him
playing an old recording of you speaking and how
your voice just smashed through the air and sort of
made me lissen like a good guitar chord can - then i
started reading about you and sort of found a friend
in you -
like - sounds a bit wanky i know - but they said
were a great man cared for others and wanted to
fucking do something - not just fucking talk and
ave meetings but actually do something - same as
my dad really - same - started the fucking hospitals
they said - we fucking need a hospital now i can tell
you - this IS the point of need... but they've sold
your dream Nye - to the highest fucking bidder
i'm sorry Nye - sorry for what we've done to your
dream - i'm sorry - an these fucking stones stood up
yer year after year where nothing grows but the
heather against against the wind - yer in the pissing

rain jus' waiting just fucking waiting for another
bastard voice to speak to raise its soul to the fucking
stars - o god - speak you bastards speak *(screams)*
speak - we - we we need your tongue for a
stammering time o god speak - you bastard speak -
(screams) speak!!
Do you know they say that up yer at night if you
look downa valley overthere, the streetlamps make
the pattern of the dragon - yeah - really now - if
you squint your eyes a bit - they ravaged all the
valleys and gave us mines then they got rid of all the
mines and now they give us factories - they'll get rid
of those and the mountains will still be yer Nye -
still be fucking yer - they'll never take those but,
but they're winning Nye they're winning - tell me
Nye would you go and kill that bastard
Worthington - would you - there's thousands like
him you see and they have to be wiped out - have
to be - vermin - fucking vermin - do you know Nye
your words stay with me - so close so fucking close
- that is my truth, now tell me yours - *(screams)*
TELL ME YOURS -

*We hear voices and music - it is PIP, JIM and CURTIS. A
disappears.*

MUSIC: 'Rehab'
[MANCHILD]

PIP: *(almost religiously)* ah, lissen, taste the fucking air
                 man - feel it - ah, so fucking beautiful - lissen taste
                 it man can you hear it all around us mun -

*JIM and CURTIS giggle and push each other taking the piss out of
PIP.*

JIM: Come on what are you on mun - do you know i
                was watching those teletubbies the other day - they
                come on after open university inna morning so if
                i've been a bit bombed and can't sleep i get up ave
                my frosties and watch some fucking thing bout the
                english language anah like and i was watching those
                right and fucking tinky winky comes on in a fucking
                skirt right - fuck me i nearly choked on my frosties -
                fucking skirt - 'im all for equality ahah like but fuck
                me mun -

PIP: what you fuckin' - on man

CURTIS: tinkie winkie

*CINDY walks up to the three. She is dressed in national costume
but with ripped tights, run eyeliner, sleeves rolled up revealing
cuts on her arms and dried blood. She is holding the doll very
tenderly. The three look round to see her standing there.*

PIP: wha the fuck is this - um uh um - CINDY - it's
                fucking Cindy -

JIM: Cind, how are you like - ok - wha' ya doin all
                dressed up like tha' for like - it's not fucking
                alloween isit -fuck me that's come quickly -

CURTIS: looks smart anyway Cind - lady in red is look -

JIM and PIP:

                Chris De Burgh - know tha' one -

CURTIS: fuck up mun -

JIM: 'aven't yerd of tha' one Curt -

CURTIS: bollocks

CINDY: no, its not halloween, its St.David's Day - St

fucking David's Day - 'aven't you ever seen a girl in national costume before say aven't you?

PIP: When we were little p'raps - but why are you dressed up like tha' then - wiv your eyes like A's - and wha's wiv the doll -

CURTIS: You are pure you are snow we are the useless sluts that they mould -

CINDY: jus felt like it - for a fucking change - and the doll is special ok - now give me some stuff ok - stop fucking about Pip - i didn't come yer for the benefit of my health ok - come on -

JIM: yeah - come on Pip -

PIP: piss off, pisss aff willya - you'll get it now *(fumbles around for gear)* and now - for the lady - here you are madam - would madam like to sample the product -

(the others giggle and laugh)

CINDY: bollocks jus' give it to me ok - *(tightens lace around her arm and injects herself, inhales deeply)*
ahh - fucking beautiful - like a permanent orgasm - yeah - fuck these stones look so beautiful i want them inside me -

JIM: My turn

CURTIS: wha about me mun - i was next -

PIP: ok ok ok wait your fucking turn *(injects himself)* - tha's better-

CINDY: do you know *(twirling around)* do you know *(off the subject)* - those fucking stars up there are fucking shiny aren't they?

JIM: know wha?

CINDY: um, dunno - oh yeah - do you know Aneurin Bevan used to cum up yer and speak to hundreds of people -

PIP: who the fuck is *(overpronounces)* - AN   NYE
RAN   BEV   AN - who the fuck was he - why
did he cum yer for - couldn't he 'ave phoned am all
-

JIM: A wuz onabout him - poet wan' 'e?

CINDY: shut up boys - he used to speak up yer, A said-

PIP: bout wha'?

JIM: sounds like fucking mesteck meg or summat - did
they 'ave the lottery in 'ose days say?

PIP: fuck up willya

JIM: release the balls...

CINDY: anyway - funny to think he was up yer years ago like
an' hundreds thousands of people would be around
lissening to 'im like - bout life politics an' stuff -

JIM: big deal who gives a toss anyway -

PIP: yeah - if they'd put a fucking big fuck off beer tent
up yer inna summer people'd come up - does he
still do it?

CURTIS: Are we too tired to try an' understand -

CINDY: nah - been dead for years - but they 'ad these stones
erected

(The three giggle like schoolboys)

PIP: wassah 'en Cind - say it again - i di'n't quite catch it
like - bout the stones like -

CINDY: they 'ad these stones put up after 'im like - to
honour him -

(JIM proceeds to urinate against one of them)

and now look what you're doing to 'em - come on
mun for fuck's sake stop it - *(pushes JIM who pisses
over himself)*

JIM: oh fucking 'ell mun - now look wha' you've done -
bollocks - aw look my batteries are fucking soaked

	now -
CINDY:	shouldn't desecrate a national monument then -
PIP:	wha' - national monument - bollocks - coupla fucking stones uppona hill - fucking hell mun - look i bet i could push the fuckers over if i wanted - *(Tries to push one over)*
CINDY:	doubt it moron -
JIM:	go on ma son - go on 'en -
CURTIS:	we love the winter it brings us closer together
PIP:	whassamatta Cind - wan' sum?
CURTIS:	my my hey hey out of the black and into the black
PIP:	- hey boys they say you can see the Welsh dragon downa valley from yer like - fucking wild innit -
JIM:	thas not a dragon it's a fucking donkey
PIP:	hey Cind does your little doll wan' sum -
CINDY:	i can't believe you fucking said tha' - fuck up right -
PIP:	alright miss fucking moral -
JIM:	thas too many temazes for you Pip, fucking dragons - what next you'll be seeing fucking Merlin next - oh fuck i 'ad a terrible fucking pain 'en - fucking stabbing like -
PIP:	ah - get on with it you fucking poofter - ave another obe - that'll sort you out -
CURTIS:	*(screams)* ah ah ah ah 1 2 3 4
PIP:	you will if you don't fuck up - you'll have the cops out yer mun -
JIM:	chill it Pip he was only singing mun -
PIP:	*(aggressively)* what did you say wanker?
JIM:	i jus' said relax mun - he was only singing - ok
PIP:	fuck off will you fuck off you wanker -
CURTIS:	there are many things that i would like to say to you
PIP:	shutit please - or i'll -

JIM goes up to Pip face to face -

JIM: jus be quiet ok - leave it *(points and jabs finger at PIP)*

PIP: stop tha' ok stop fucking tha' -

JIM: alright - stop - for fuck's sake let's stop it mun - right -

CURTIS: you gonna be the one that saves me - an all the roads we walk are blind -

Jim suddenly clasps his chest, goes white and slumps to the floor against the stone that he pissed against. Everyone stops and freezes-

PIP: come on Jim stop pissing about mun - will you - come on -

CURTIS: star bright keep me safe today and tonight

CINDY: Jim, are you ok - Jim - are you ok - say - Jim - JIM!!

PIP: fuck - are you ok Jim - say *(goes up to him and slaps him in the face - no response - tries to move him but he is a dead weight)*
          Jim - wassamatta say - fucking hell quick get an ambulance - will someone get a fucking ambulance -

CINDY: - he's fucking dying - go an get help - quick - for fuck's sake-please -

CURTIS: in the beginning, when we were winning when our smiles were genuine -

CINDY: oh curtis, fucking 'ell wha' we gonna do what we gonna do *(holds JIM and her doll)* - speak to me Curt - fucking speak to me -

PIP: fuck me - i'm off - i'm i'm - i'm off to get help ok - off to get help - hang on - ok

PIP runs off.

CINDY: curtis don't go
CURTIS: i i i - i gotta g go
CINDY: don't fucking go please - speak mun speak to me
            please *(pleading)*
CURTIS: is anyone going anywhere
CINDY: oh curtis fuck up fuck up mun please can't you see
            open your eyes see what the fuck's going on mun -
            look!!!
CURTIS: we all face the same way
CINDY: you can't go on like this mun - look Jim is yer
            fucking dying and you're fucking jabbering help me
            curtis - speak speak *(He goes)*
CINDY: No you bastard no - it's all going going going -
            please

CINDY is left crouched with JIM whispering words and singing to him-

CINDY: well fucking great - nice night out - i hope they've
            got help or we're fucked Jim - really fucked-
            fucking great - take it away take it all fucking away -
            stop this feeling stop this pain please please take it
            all away - Jim Jim-where the fuck are you - Jim -
            i'm invisible, invisible as air - i'm, i'm not here -
            gone gone gone - it's not hurting anymore - you
            can't get to me anymore, anymore - *(holds the
            doll,blood drips)* my love, my love - fucking world -
            fucking place - *(looks up)* soothe me someone
            something - *(whispers)* stars stars can you hear me
            can you see me can you feel this - can you hear my

heart beat, beating, beat, beaten - twinkle twinkle
little star how i wonder what you are - twinkle
twinkle little star - fuck it fuck it you're all dead up
there aren't you - bright and burning - so so far
away - but you're all dead... dead dead - Jim Jim -
Jim - something, something must grow -

(Adresses the audience)

look, look Jim is dying - Jim is fucking dying up yer
under the sky the beautiful sky - he's dying an what
can i you anyone do - what can i do say say? the
whole world is dying - even the stars have given up
- seen too much - - what can i do what can you do
Mr Bevan - where are you now - now when we
need you when we really fucking need you - say -
say - can't you yer me say - you bastard you fucking
bastard - look take a look at this land of my fathers
land of my fucking fathers hey hey - take a look -
fuck your dragon burn your flag fuck your langauge
boil your leeks destroy the welsh assembly cut your
daffodils - fuck it all fuck it all - we've lost it's all
gone - gone gone gone - nos da nos da no stars no
stars nos da cariad cariad my baby my baby *(picks up
the doll, cradles it)* where are you now? nos da cariad
- nos da - no stars - no -
you can't touch me anymore you bastards - sorry all
gone gone gone - nowhere now all gone - scattered
flowers in the rain, in the rain - going going gone
you bastards - i wanna slow down to a zero i wanna
go now - now now - fade fade fade away - Curt
Curt where are you - can't you hear me Curt, Curt
- so damn easy to cave in man man kills everything -

She continues to rip up her clothes - her flesh is a mess of scars and

lines set against gentle pure whitechalk skin - she is left standing
hysterical and naked and pours the bleach into her mouth

> you you can't reach me anymore - i am your
> sacrifice we we are your sacrifice - i'm with the stars
> now - i'm with my baby, my perfect pure baby, i'm
> free, i'm me - - nos da nos da - nos

CINDY collapses next to JIM and the half buried doll.
Wind. Then silence.

ACT 2

UNIT 14

MUSIC: 'The Everlasting'
[MANIC STREET PREACHERS]

A, PIP and CURTIS are at JIM's grave. Silence.
The word DISEASE is sprayed onto the back wall.

UNIT 15

THE GAP THAT GROWS BETWEEN OUR LIVES THE
GAP OUR PARENTS NEVER HAD STOP THOSE
THOUGHTS CONTROL YOUR MIND REPLACE THE
THINGS THAT YOU DESPISE OH YOU'RE OLD I HEAR
YOU SAY IT DOESNT MEAN THAT I DON'T CARE I
DON'T BELIEVE IN IT ANYMORE PATHETIC ACTS FOR
A WORTHLESS CAUSE

IN THE BEGINNING WHEN WE WERE WINNING WHEN
OUR SMILES WERE GENUINE IN THE BEGINNING

WHEN WE WERE WINNING WHEN OUR SMILES WERE
GENUINE BUT NOW UNFORGIVEN THE EVERLASTING
EVERLASTING

NARRATOR:

so - another statistic another petalled sympathy
another joyrider another drug victim another off
the dole register another dead soul rising to the
stars above - another loss another victory another
and another and another - so - here we are another
funeral another WH fucking Auden poem another
torn mind to heal - so it goes and on it goes - time -
time to withdraw hide away stay inside for lent and
pretend it doesn't hurt is it - we walk with the
cemetry we lissen to the graves speak to us - inside
us and out - we - we are the fallen the un the dis
the the wept generation even though it is too much
to expect a tear - we commune with the ghosts of
forever - acned faces pushed tight against mortuary
glass - no life lived - gone - wiped out like
sandcastles upon a beach gone going gone - forever
- left staring at the sun the sad setting sun - my son
my son - i see the vultures circling above waiting
waiting for another to give up - fall - collapse - we
try we try to live on an earth that weeps daily - but
there are no bandages for the scars - the scars -
child molester paedophilliac web found self
castration on the internet fistfuck tummy tuck
murder your gran say you were smacked as a child
watch tv feel free feel you were right to kill - suck in

the headlines and head for notoriety - lithium
prozac viagra zispin temazepam diazepam amyl
nitrate valium cocaine propane petrol novacaine
methadone metronomes to absolve your sins -
speak on oprah springer lake and kilroy the time the
place it'll be ok it'll be safe - find yourself another
couch babe and you'll get through - we endure we
endure - black nights and sunscorched days -
further further away - life is a placebo life is cracking
life is pot life is shit - life is in search of heroes - life
is dying dying - it could be you doesn't necessarily
mean winning the fucking lottery - yeah yeah yeah -
so - we resume we fade we are holy we are full of
holes - need something to fill them in - don't give
me a shovel or i'll dig my grave - i am an architect
they call me a butcher i am purity they call me
perverted i am soil they call me soiled - the sun
breaks black over the horizon the leaves turn green
on the trees - the soul waits the soul waits;

UNIT 16

MUSIC: 'Faster'
[MANIC STREET PREACHERS]

Bright lights on the stage - clinical white.
The word SQUALOR is splashed on the back wall.

UNIT 17

MUSIC: 'Design for Life' instrumental
[MANIC STREET PREACHERS]

CINDY: yeah - keep us down paint us a mountain-top and
leave us to fight it fucking out - fight and fuck let us
stutter and crack let us kill each other over a fucking
parking space outside the spar
Leave us to work but to constantly owe - owe - owe
leave us to moan about next door's carpet and
laugh as we scratch at our scratch cards and dream
of early retirement - call us lazy cos we won't take
any job but you try getting up at 7 to go the
japcunt factory downa valley where they pay us 20
quid more than onna dole and have to lissen to
those wankers all day - call us lazy - i call tha'
principles you cunts -
I - have - never - seen - my - dad   work
work
So judge deny defy hate mistrust point the finger
burn rob rape ravage castrate laugh at lay seige to
E   rad   i   cate
But remember we are breathing
we are not alone you think we are think we are all
too fucked up selfish thick lotteried up off our
heads on crack cocaine but we're not and one day
we're gonna find our voice then BOOM
BOOM
middle 'en - ger - land take a fucking look
BOOM
we are a living exhibition of how not to be
BOOM
one day we are going to find our voice
BOOM
We are nothing and should be everything
BOOM
and

one day
you will know the meaning of
E   RAD   I   CATE
BOOM
day one

UNIT 18

*The factory. The men and women are working at their machines
and Worthington is in his office at the end of the stage. The
workers cannot see inside. They will continue working as the
scene progresses. A enters the factory floor then walks down the
line and knocks on the door to Worthington's office.*

WORTHINGTON:

Come in, sit down. Did you bring your cv? What is
it you are interested in here - is it production line -
we have one vacancy there - have you had
experience? By the way sonny we don't allow make-
up for the men here -

A: Oh yes, plenty of experience - i am very well
acquainted with the factory floor and the
production line - oh yes, very well, i know a lot -
it's not make-up by the way - i can see clearer with
it on -

WORTHINGTON:

We'll see about that - have you actually worked on
one - do you know how it works?

A: yes, indeed

WORTHINGTON:

where - is it on your cv? look - we really have to
move along - why do you want to work here?

A: Oh, of course - i won't keep you a minute sir - just

bear with me for a moment - it will be worth your
while Mr Worthington - please - i won't keep you -
and of course i do realise you have prior
commitments - of course - ah,what was the
question again?

WORTHINGTON:

why do you want to work here - ?

A: saw you in the paper - givin' that cheque to charity
- nice gesture if i may say -

WORTHINGTON:

well -

A: um, let me see - yeah,right - i love production line
work and i am honest, an excellent timekeeper,
enjoy working as a team and on my own and feel
that this company does a lot to promote human
endeavours -

WORTHINGTON:

(looking surprised) oh - yes - um er well, very good -
well - what would you say is the most important
attribute to working in a factory such as ours then
young man?

A: oh, as i said - honesty, virtue, a belief in the future -
basically to give your all to the company as of
course i would - anything else?

WORTHINGTON:

um, well - i must say you sound a perfect candidate
for the post - how would you get to work - we do
have to ask these things you understand - i mean
could we depend on you?

A: oh of course i understand - i drive a push bike and
live right next door to a brand new bus stop and, of
course you could depend on me -

WORTHINGTON:

right, well then *(looks at watch)* i have a few more
candidates to see tommorow - so - Mr - er um sorry
- what did you say your name was Mr um - ?

A: oh - it's Dai - aye - Dai Cunt -

WORTHINGTON:

excuse me - did you say David - David Cunt - is
that right say - Mr Cunt?

A: *(laughs)* no, i said Dai di as in lady - bless her soul -
do you know tha' really hurt me - so sad so fucking
sad -

WORTHINGTON:

yes - i know but what's it got to do with the
interview Mr - Mr Cunt?

A: nah - i said it's di, it's DI CUNT -

*WORTHINGTON starts to look worried and irritated - he goes
to use the phone - A pulls cable out of telephone*

WORTHINGTON:

why - why - why did you do that - i'll have to call
security if you don't leave this office right now - i
thought you said you came here for an interview -
for the production line?

A: yes, that's right - so did i get the job - say? did i
fucking get it?

WORTHINGTON:

well, if you leave right now i will consider your
application *(goes to get up)*

A: sit right back please Mr Worthington - you're not
going anywhere - i am fucking security - now you
jus' sit down and we'll have that little interview -
can we? please calm down and make yourself
comfortable -

WORTHINGTON:

>now look here young man i don't know what you
>want - do you care for to leave now -

A:

>- fucking shut up you bastard - sit down - and
>lissen fucking lissen - shut.your.mouth. your dirty
>rat infested money ruled gob and lissen to me ok o
>fuckin' k you're not going anywhere ok -

WORTHINGTON:

>wh - wh - why - why should i - what is this all about
>- can't we sort this out in a more civilised manner?

A:

>yeah yeah yeah - jus' like you treat people is it Mr
>fucking Worthington - just like you treat people -
>with decency care and attention - eh eh eh you
>bastard - well *(shouts)* ACHTUNG!!!!

WORTHINGTON:

>*(frightened, shaking)* i i i i don't know what you're
>talking about - what d d do you you mean - I don't
>think I can give you that job now

A:

>*(paces around)* do you remember a man, a man who
>used to work - if that's what you call it - here, oh
>about a year ago - Bill Jones - does it ring a bell eh
>Mr Worthington?

WORTHINGTON:

>uh, can't recall that - um - Jones - we we have so
>many jones here -

A:

>Bill Jones - can't have had too many of those
>though i presume - come on come on - try an
>remember can you - can you?

WORTHINGTON:

>i'm thinking - no - can't seem to put a face to the
>name - how long did he work here for - couple of
>months - weeks - um -

A:

>shut the fuck up wanker - Bill Jones worked here

for 10 bastard years - never missed a day of work -
always on time - packing department - now do you
remember him? hey come on come on -

WORTHINGTON:

um, sorry still can't picture him - why?

A:
why - why - WHY!! why - because he's my dad and
you sacked him, you made him *(over emphasizes)* re
dun   dant - you humanly shed him you helped
him on his merry way - yes, Mr worthy
Worthington - you gave him the push - now. now
do you remember him - my dad - Bill Jones - see
any resemblance say - go on *(gets closer)* go on have
a look - have a good fucking look - see? *(gets out a
stanley knife)*

WORTHINGTON:

(worried - seeing what's going on now) yeah yeah - i
think i do remember him now - good - good
worker - quiet - yes,of course i remember William
now - *(trying to get out of it)* - oh yes -

A:
good, very good - well you should - you sacked him
- why? do you remember - and the name is Bill ok?

WORTHINGTON:

yes, i'm sorry - Bill yes of course - well, people
come and go so often it's hard to remember - but i
think it was in the time when we didn't have
enough work on - yes, that's it - happy now - can i
go now?

A:
oh, of course - that's it - off the fucking hook now
aren't you? walk right out - freedom tastes sweet
doesn't it - no - actually you can't - it's only just
begun -

WORTHINGTON:

but what more is there to say - i'm sorry if there was

a problem but it was a difficult time for all of us -
what more can i say - business is business -

A: business is business is it - no it's not - life is life
money is money - life is death - greed is greed then
- people are people - all removeables aren't we -
passing always - work is work - come and go - all
removeables - come an go - work then leave then
die - eh you bastard - how dare you *(stares him in
the face)* how the fuck dare you choose people's
lives - do you know my friend is dead and my best
friend is on a life support machine and cunts like
you are sat in cunts like this twiddling your thumbs
waiting for five o clock to come so you can go and
get a special massage by some Chinese girl who'll
let you stick your dick in her armpit - fucking
nothing - you are a nobody - with your mobile
phone your holiday home and pension scheme - ah,
fuck off -

WORTHINGTON:
i've got money if that's what you want - lots of it -
perhaps you could take your dad out somewhere
nice or something - look *(opens wallet - money falls
out)*

A scumples it up and chews one, then spits it out -

A: tastes good eh - freedom tastes so fucking good -
you will stay yer until i deem you no longer fucking
necessary -

WORTHINGTON:
people will miss me and come looking - then you'll
be in trouble - all my workers are just outside my
office - look i'm prepared to forget all this if you let

me go ok - i can't be fairer than that can i - can i?

A: always the one, the fucking one doing a favour eh
          eh - no - not this time ok - we won't forget it ok -
          and i'm doing you a favour right - i'm in charge

WORTHINGTON:

          what do you want - look it's finishing time soon
          and my workers will come in to the office -

A: i want you to know what it's like to be controlled
          by another's hand - i want you to feel fear to know
          what it's like to not know what's gonna happen
          next - ok - not nice is it - go on fucker - plead -
          make my fucking day - do you know i love that film
          Taxidriver - wipe the scum off the earth - are you
          talking to me? are YOU talking to ME!! say -
          answer scum cos that's what you are see scum -
          scum with a capital F - DI CUNT DI CUNT - *(A
          cuts the tops of Worthington's fingertips)*

WORTHINGTON:

          aarrgh - shit - god

A: god - do you think there even is a god up there - i
          tell you he's fucked off a long time ago - and i
          don't think he'd lissen to cunts like you - so shut
          the fuck up - now - try working the line now - they
          won't help you anyway - off home now -

A pulls out a gun, an old fashioned pistol

WORTHINGTON:

          look, there's nothing i can do now - look - i'm only
          doing my job - i i i used to be like you - i worked
          my way up - got 2 kids and a mortgage to pay for -
          i i i'm only doing what i'm told - there's always
          someone telling me what to do - i don't have a

choice - i do it or i'm gone - see - i was just doing
what i was told to do - i'm sorry sonny - i said i'm
sorry sonny - please put the gun away - please?

A: sonny fucking sonny - who do you think you are -
how many other lives have you destroyed - say -
say? how many you stupid fucker - hundreds
families souls how many - you've got fucking blood
on your hands and i'm yer to even up the balance -
and you do have a choice - we all have a fucking
choice - right -

WORTHINGTON:

ok ok

A: look, here's a picture of my dad - go on - have a
good look - might refresh your septic mind - *(hands
photo)* ring a bell - big fella - wasn't afraid of
anything - 'cept losing his job - so his family would
be ok - see -

WORTHINGTON:

oh, yes - i can remember him now - Jones - Jerry -
yes - good - good worker - Jerry - i mean William -
yes - William Jones - yes -

A: fuck you fuck you - what do you know or care jus'
another piece of meat jus' another to fuck up -

A: see this gun - it was my grandad's - he went off
from yer to fight the fascists in Spain - know wha' a
fascist is eh? should do - anyway he called it his
poetry - his beatiful poetry - said he was gonna
teach them fascists a lesson - make 'em lissen to
some good old fashioned Welsh poetry he said - aye
- nice innit - oh aye - do you know who Aneurin b
Bevan was -

WORTHINGTON:

who do you think you are you and your generation

with your cars and attitude what have you ever
done what do you know about Aneurin Bevan
you're a pervert a zero

A: fuck up - he he was a good man - a good good man
who cared about people - set up the nhs he did -
know wha' tha' is you bupa'd bastard eh? said he
was gonna change the world said tha' he was going
to *(over does)* E - RAD - I - CATE want disease
ignorance idleness and squalor - well he didn't quite
do tha' cos of cunts like you but anyway - he hated
tories he did - know wha' they are? he really hated
them and he said - see - those men who are
marching off to fight the fascists in Spain - well,
you'd better watch cos one day they gonna turn on
those fascists at home - he said - so. so - yer we are -
i got the gun and you need the fucking hospital -
(A puts gun in Worthington's mouth) good old Nye
- knew wha' he was talking about - so i think it's
time - i think it's time - di cunt di - you're not
worth fucking bovering with - go on go on fuck off
- fuck off outta yer - you'll never understand - and
this black is yer for a fucking reason - right - *(head
in hands crying - eyeliner runs all over his face)*

WORTHINGTON:
            right, ok ok it's just life - isn't it? It's just life,
sonny.

*Just as A fires the gun the factory hooter sounds and the workers get
up from their machines and stretch. Worthington falls to the
ground.*

A: the sun riseth and the sun setteth - to all things
have a beginning and an ending the wind bloweth

east and the wind bloweth west - all things shall
return - nothing is original under the sun - the wind
bloweth and all returneth to its place of origin -
(mutters) i gotta go and tell dad - i gotta go and tell
dad - tell dad its over - it's over now - he's gone,
gone - all over now -

*A walks out of the door muttering to himself - out past the line as
the workers pack up their stuff to leave - no one notices Worthington
as blood seeps through his office spreading over the floor.*

UNIT 19

MUSIC: 'Everything Must Go'
[MANIC STREET PREACHERS]

PIP and CURTIS are sat in the park which is bleak.

PIP: don't know wha' to say really -
CURTIS: bout wha' -
PIP: bout everything - Cindy and Jim - it all it fucking all
             - don't know mun -
CURTIS: all i wanna to do is live no matter how miserable it
             is -
PIP: what - off again eh?
CURTIS: yeah, s'pose - that's all we got sumtimes - words
             words - where do we go from yer?
PIP: home isit?
CURTIS: i really miss Cind and Jim mun - i really fucking do
             - why did it ave to appen mun Pip - jus' like ah
             uppona fuckin' hill - do you think A's right?
PIP: bout wha?
CURTIS: bout life an all tha' - work life Wales

everyfuckingthing mun - i used to like you and him
arguing and stuff - great like -

PIP: Curt - thassa most i yerd you say for fucking years
mun - why -

CURTIS: fucking teachers an stuff - libraries gave us power -

PIP: sumtimes i agreed wiv him like but he used to go
on and on like - jus' made my ead spin - i mean
we're all fucked ain we - all fucked - look at this
fucking place mun - fucking eats souls like fuck - i
know that i don't need some fucking cunt of a
university professor to come an analyse me an my
place do i - i know i fucking know -

CURTIS: he's no professor mun - jus' liked his books - think i
might go an see Cind - someone said they're after
us but they won't be up there willaye?

PIP: nah - doubt it mun -

CURTIS: we gotta carry each other, carry each other - i'll take
a picture of you to remember how good you looked
-

*A comes running up to the park. He is out of breath, flushed,
excited, confused - he stops - holding the gun.*

PIP: fucking hell where ave you been -

CURTIS: whas the gun for - gonna hold up the post office
eh? everything must go and i hope that you'll
forgive us but everything must go -

A: i did it - i fucking did it - killed the bastard - he's
gone - gone - ha ha - yes -

PIP: you are fucking mad - A what have you done -
really - you killed tha' bloke inna factree - fucking
hell - you're madder than i thought -

CURTIS: if you stand up like a nail you will be knocked down

A: i feel fucking great mun - i feel fucking free -

PIP: no preaching now isit - jus' kill the fuckers - come
           on mun A you can't go on like this can you?

A: why not - there's plenty more like him mun -
           waiting for it -

PIP: what you gonna do now - can't stay yer waving tha'
           fucking thing bout can you?

CURTIS: what I would give for just one of your smiles, one
           of your smiles

A: see - i knew i knew it was the right thing to do - do
           you know - when i was in there wiv 'im i had power
           i had the power i had what he always used - i had it
           and he couldn't do a fucking thing about it -

PIP: cunts sacked me today as well jus' cos i went to
           Jim's funeral and didn't tell 'em - fuck 'em -
           couldn't give a toss -

A: see Pip it's everywhere mun - all the same - we're all
           on our knees hoping it's not our turn - fucking
           scared - so wha' we gonna do mun - gotta do
           sumthing - an after all tha' wiv Cind and Jim i
           thought fuck it - the time has come -

CURTIS: I'm tired of giving a reason when the future is what
           we believe in

PIP: i jus' might fuck off from roun yer - nick a merc and
           gone - like the fucking wind - ram a chemist get a
           load of e or summat and fuck - off uppa motorway -
           gone mun -

A: why run?

PIP: sick of it mun - what's left - best mate gone -
           fucking Cind on a life support machine - what else?

A: why not do sumthing like - start a fucking war
           mun?

PIP: don't fucking start now mun - right -

CURTIS: we'll be together till the end - for now and forever -

A: i did it - i fucking did it - knew it'd be the right thing -

PIP: but the fucking cops'll catch you - what you gonna do then say? its not gonna work A - we're still all fucking losers fucking dead lives ain't gonna come alive jus' like ah mun - we're jus' stuck and so hope forra bit of fun bit of escape bit of fucking life nowanagain mun -

CURTIS: take my hand and together we will cry

A: why not - look mun - we gotta - fuck me - Cind in a bastard coma and Jim fucking dead - and what for - we gotta try mun - fucking Aneurin Bevan fucking chartists fucking welsh brigade fucking poets fucking bands still still gotta -

CURTIS: say where is the tomorrow -

A: try mun - there is still power left inus mun - so much still to do - so much

PIP: come on mun A jus' cos you killed some bloke you think the fucking revolution is coming - grow up - look don't get me fucking angry now - ok

CURTIS: don't leave me high don't leave me dry don't leave me -

A: Pip mun - please - i feel it's not over yet - there's so much work to do so much shit to sort out - still so much scum to wipe out - tha's why i wear this *(points to his eyes)* to never give in -

CURTIS: just like an old man's dreams -

PIP: wha' do you mean? look A i jus' think i might go an nick a fuckingmerc and go go go -

A: i wear it cos of my dad when he used to come home from work downa pit and he used to say he could see through the dark with it - and it always made

	me feel safe - victory is ackowledging the fact we have not yet lost -
CURTIS:	just take a look at the whites of my eyes -
PIP:	see A you are fucking mad mun - but i gotta give it to you you did it - you fucking did it mun - come on Curt let's leave trotsky - fancy a spin?
CURTIS:	i'm fucked with being fucked i'm done with being dumb, being dumb
A:	that's my truth - now tell me yours - tell me yours -
CURTIS:	i'm going to see how Cindy is ok - see you after - and we are told that this is the end -
A:	see you - take care Curt - give her this will you -

A hands Curt a picture of them as kids, he looks at it.

CURTIS:	fuck me i haven't seen tha' for years - look at tha' haircut mun!!
PIP:	less ave a look mun - mad mun - they were the days eh?
CURTIS:	in the beginning when we were winning when our smiles were genuine -

CURTIS walks off slowly.

PIP:	you should be on telly with all those quotes mun - do you know i almost fucking like you in some strange fuckoff sort of way - like i said i like you cos you aven't given in and mow your lawn on sunday or snort coke downa rugby club - instead we're stood yer talking about how you you've killed some cunt of a human resource manager - oh A what you gonna do mun -
A:	carry on - don't care now - it's like a book -

PIP: don't start on the books and stuff - killing yeah - but no fucking books ok -

A: ok ok

PIP: one day we'll do summat together eh?

A: sure you won't kill me first

PIP: what about Cind and Jim what a fuckin' waste - they don't know if she's gonna come out of the coma - i haven't told Curt -

PIP: what the fuck we gonna do mun?

A: i know - i i i i don't fucking know - i don't know who is the bastard enemy anymore - you hate as much as me don't you Pip?

PIP: for love - for love -

A: yes - i know - for something better - something better'n'this - love - yeah -

PIP: inna way - but i jus' aven't got the brain - jus' wanna drive fast get away - we'll do summat together one day - ok ok A do it together one day - you're fucking mad you are -

A: no fear - no fucking fear - we'll beat the whole fucking world - see—i i i i gotta go an see dad - i i i gotta go an tell him -

PIP: take care - alright A - a i'll nick a car and you can write a fucking book about it yeah?

A: *(suddenly realises what's happened)* yeah yeah - i gotta go now gotta go an talk to dad -

PIP and A both exit the stage.

UNIT 20

MUSIC: 'My Selfish Gene'
[CATATONIA]

An intensive care room. CINDY is laying in bed with tubes going in and out of her. CURTIS is pacing up and down. A single vase of daffodils on a white locker. A green blanket on the edge of the bed.

CURTIS: Cin,C C C Cin Cindy - it's it's Curtis yer - jus' popped by to say hello and to hold hold your hand like - *(pause)* are are are you ok - i'm sorry about all these wires and tubes and stuff it's horrible to see you like this Cind - you were always on the rampage - - i i i don't know wha' to say really - i feel like going back to my song lyrics - feel safe there - - Cind - it's gonna be alright - you mustn't give up ok - mustn't - all these tubes an things - fuck 'em Cind - oh sorry for swearing - oh bollocks - why not - they are not what's keeping you alive Cind - fuck no - no - it's your heart it's your fucking heart your soul your eyes your hands your mind keeping you going - it is Cind - it fucking is mun - i can feel you in there even though you are sleeping - you are her mun - you are here Cind ok - *(gets closer and looks deeper into her closed eyes)* Cind - we we we should have kept our baby we really should have i i i i know it was the wrong time - i i i'm so sorry but we should have and we could have had tha' little flat and it would have been alright - i'm sorry i let you down - but we can still make it alright - we can Cind - we can - give - give me a sign Cind - Cind you are not ready for drowning - you are not ok - not now not like this not by THEM THEM ok ok ok - you're not ready for drowning - we have to go on and on and on...

enter Pip, Jim and A

A:	we are not deceived by your words
PIP:	whose fucking words?
A:	We see through your promises
JIM:	promised us the earth
CINDY:	taken my faith away
A:	we are the disaffected
CURTIS:	the lipless screaming
CINDY:	i cut i tear i burn i am i am alive
PIP:	shopping doesn't make me happy
JIM:	all property is theft
CURTIS:	a memory or dream
CINDY:	a scratch or a scream
	this hole in my throat
CURTIS:	allow me to speak
PIP:	this place without meaning
JIM:	this stuttering eloquence of screaming
A:	so save us all allow desolation
PIP:	find a path be unafraid to act
A:	stand stand oak tall even the smallest body makes a
CURTIS:	shadow
CINDY:	we are butterflies trapped in the frost
PIP:	victory is acknowledging the fact that we, we have not yet lost
A:	lost
JIM:	so caress me with you alienation
CINDY:	alienate me with your caress
PIP:	create me with your credit
A:	pour me power through direct debit
CURITS:	feed me freedom
PIP:	from selling shares
A:	we

	We are the industrial tribunals
JIM:	the penny pinchers super savers
PIP:	lottery watchers
CURTIS:	we are the incoherent throats searching for sound
CINDY:	the peaceful protestor
	the single mother
A:	we
PIP:	we are the denied
A:	yet unified
JIM:	we are the tapestry
CURTIS:	the words they try to deny us
PIP:	dislocated desperations
CINDY:	stitched
A:	together
CURIS:	by the disparate verses of our
CINDY:	skin
A:	we are the sound
CURTIS:	the silence
A:	the sound
ALL:	of the alone to the alone
PIP:	of the ability to resist
A:	and in
PIP:	our
CURTIS:	voices
CINDY:	the milk of a mother
PIP:	against against
JIM:	their chains that smother
CINDY:	mother to man to woman to child
CURTIS:	this desperate scream
PIP:	spread nationwide
CURTIS:	and in this
PIP:	division
ALL:	there is a unity

A: and

CINDY: in this incision there is a sanctity

A: and in this societal mind cage

CINDY: blisters

PIP: a cacophony *(enraged)*

A: with the burn of generations following the bullet of
                emancipation

ALL: we are
             the breaking
             we are we are
             the making
             we are we are
             the ripping
             we are we are
             the stitching
             a NO in search of a YES
             we are we are

A: everything

ALL: the making
             we are we are

A: must

ALL: we are we are
             the blind beginning to see

A: go

*Curtis falls on Cindy, desperate, sobbing, holding her - a stand falls
over, tubes pull out, a bag of blood spills and tips all over the
floor - factory hooter goes off - chaos - nurses rush in try and
grab Curtis who is clinging to Cindy - she grabs his hand really
tightly but the nurses don't see this - so continue to tear him off
- they manage to extract him from Cindy and bundle him away
from her to the side of the room as he shouts and protests.*

NURSE: get him out of here, get him out

CURTIS: she's awake - get a doctor or something she's not
            going to die - she held my hand - she's going to be
            alright - she held my hand

NURSE: get him out she hasn't moved all day - she's just
            another stupid self-harmer that went wrong - just
            get him out -

CURTIS: what the fuck? She held my fucking hand I felt her -
            Cind hold on - you're not ready for drowning
            you're not - Cind hold on hold on - I'm going to
            tell the others ok please please hold on -

*CURTIS exits the stage, the nurses grudgingly comfort CINDY
as the lights dim -*

UNIT 21

NARRATOR:

            the 5th and final word. IDLENESS is splashed onto
            the back wall. We can now see the five words clearly
            -

*MUSIC: 'The Everlasting' instrumental
[MANIC STREET PREACHERS]*

NARRATOR:

            once upon a time
            when work meant something when there was a
            dignity to what we left for not now this slavery they
            call the free market economy - the bosses and the
            bossed the them and the us the fucked and the
            fuckers except we all want to be the them - and the

working class, if there is such a thing, - thought
under the tories they could all be middle class and
so forgot about everybody else and marched to the
sound of money makers and faceless bankers but
didn't realise they were being shafted all the way
along just move people along just give the masses a
scrap and let them fight for it - idleness laziness
unemployment redundant - tory or new labour they
love these words - gives them power gives them a
reason to be to to to to tell us how we are and what
we should be be be BE. But, as Aneurin Bevan said
- "the verb is more important than the noun" - see
- we like our words too - too and how i feel so idle
as i make tea for some company meeting or how
unemployed i feel as i insert a metal object into
some cunt of a Korean box or how redundant i am
as i talk to my new deal adviser about the future and
to have time on one's hands to watch the stars to
breathe the wind to read a book to throw a brick
how useless - what inertia drugs me as i stare at the
job cards at the job centre £3.60 per hour rising to
£3.78 after 6 months, after 6 months -
how vegetating i become when i guide the newest
group of cameraclad japtourists down the model of
a pit, of a pit -
how inactive i feel when you ask me if i get
depressed
how i loaf how i leisure how i dilly fucking dally
how i laze
how how HOW I FUCKING BE BE BE!!
once upon a time......
then a sentence from each of the narrations

A: see,we didn't start this you know we we didn't start this fucking war we call living today

PIP: taste it fuck it eat it shit it smell it take it fake it cuts
my tongue and slits my wrist if i think too hard

CURTIS: prozac ain't no bandage to this much blood

CINDY: blind me with tears - cover my eyes - slice my ear
off - I don't want to hear no more -

JIM: we commune with the ghosts of forever - acned
faces pushed tight against mortuary glass

PIP: once upon a time, when........

UNIT 22

MUSIC: 'Small Black Flowers that Grow in the Sky'
[MANIC STREET PREACHERS]

Mourners enter, each carrying a cross which they place on stage.
They slowly exit as A enters.

UNIT 23

A: dad, dad, i'm here ok, it's me - sorry i haven't been
for a while but life has been busy - but i i i'm here
ok - dad - i did it - i killed Worthington - it's all
over now - he can't do it anymore - he can't - all
gone - now - it's ok though it's ok - i feel ok - in
the light dad, in the light - i can see the light now -
the darkenss has faded it's ok - dad dad i did it for
you - its ok its all gone now - peace and quiet -
peacefilled now - i can come here every day now
and talk dad - i can - just like i was little - i won't
have that pumping in my head anymore - it's all
gone - i can breathe again - i can breathe dad - the

air is clean - the night is not dark - i can see the
light - i can see - it'll be alright -
after the snow there must be the grass
after the rain there must be the tree
after life and pain maybe we are free
after the death lived
maybe we do remain we do remain
after the snow there is the grass
there is the grass ... ...
you are free dad   free

*Sirens, noise, armed policemen enter from all directions - A
doesn't attempt to run*

POLICEMAN: we are armed police do exactly as i say and you
will come to no harm - put your hands above your
head, turn round and walk towards us

A: i can be with you every day now - dad - *(pulls gun
out)* dad do you remember when we was little kids
and you'd look up into the sky and say that the first
star out was granny up there coming out to say that
she's alright - do you remember......

POLICEMAN: put your arms above your head, turn around
and walk towards us

A: dad... do you... well... i look up there every night
dad every night and she's still there... shining
shining so bright... dad... she is...

POLICEMAN: put your hands above your head, turn around
and walk towards us

A: why? i haven't done anything wrong - i am standing
in the light - i haven't done anything wrong -

POLICEMAN: gun

A: this is my truth now tell me yours

POLICEMAN: put the gun down.

A: this gun is poetry is fucking poetry - lissen - lissen to this silence - gwlad glwad pleidiol wyf 'im gwlad - to wear the scars - forever -

POLICEMAN: put the gun down sonny

A: "forever" - no such thing as forever unless there are people with the faith and belief to fight for it - forever

POLICEMAN: this isn't a game - put the gun down

A: poetry - fu ck ing poetry - can you hear it - lissen -

POLICEMAN: i said, put the fucking gun down.

Suddendly PIP and CURTIS burst on stage, the policemen are startled and aim their guns at them

PIP: don't shoot

POLICEMAN: back off

CURTIS: please - we know him -

POLICEMAN: we are armed police this is a situation you cannot win

PIP: there's been a mistake - please - he's my brother

POLICEMAN: stay back

CURTIS: his dad's calling him -

POLICEMAN: I repeat we are armed police

PIP: just let us take him home - please -

A recites the last few lines of the passage that was spoken at the beginning:

A: though foremen have trampled in triumph thy vales yet fail they to silence to silence the old tongue of wales
thy harpstrings unbroken by traitor's fell hand

	still sing to me songs of my land
	still sing to me songs of my land ... ...
PIP:	A please - you were right - we'll do summat together o k
A:	still shining dad still still...
CURTIS:	Cindy's - gonna be alright - we have to hold on, eh hold on
A:	Still shining dad
CINDY:	No more bleeding, this is my beginning, we are the tommorrow
POLICEMAN:	look A, i'll put my gun down ok *(puts his gun down onto the floor)*
A:	something must grow......something must

A puts the gun to his head ... the stage goes black ... factory hooter blasts ... silence ... a spotlight finds Pip staring at the audience ...

PIP:	these these are my scars this is my breathing it will never stop, never - this is my truth, now tell me yours -

MUSIC: 'No Surface All Feeling'
[MANIC STREET PREACHERS]

unprotected sex:

oliver ryan, maria pride, richard harrington

photograph: dave daggers

Unprotected sex

first performed in October 1999 at
The Sherman Theatre in Cardiff

director: Phil Clark
designer: Jane Linz Roberts
lighting designer: Ceri James

cast
denver: oliver ryan
gary: richard harrington
triste: maria pride

unprotected sex:
oliver ryan, maria pride, richard harrington

photograph: dave daggers

unprotected sex

scene 1

DENVER: in the mist, mist yes i see the ponies drifting drifting down from the mountain and whenever i felt alone or need to feel the air swoosh around within me i would go up there and look for them - and there'd be these two ponies that would be away from the herd - all by themselves - a lovely ragged mad brown one and a delicate gentle white one with the saddest eyes you've ever seen and i sort of made them mine up there - it was my our world up up there - i'd go up cos nobody looked after them onna mountains they just survived all by themselves and i'd see them beneath the wind and the sky together together like two old lovers outside tesco - playing and grazing together and i remember thinking how lovely it must be to belong somewhere with someone... and i'd just listen listen to the silence -
an one day i went up there and i noticed that the white one - the woman one was walking a bit slower and laying down more so i went up closer and could see that she...

GARY: do you remember Triste?

TRISTE: what when?

DENVER: memory me memoir hold the picture re-mem-ber - yes i i i remember?

GARY: remember: when we smiled when we held each other like a

TRISTE: ocean to the shore yes Gary i remember you

GARY: me

TRISTE: only had to touch you and you had a stiffy like
GARY: the Blackpool tower?
DENVER: running away away into the fields up up into the
            mountains -
TRISTE: half a packet of polos!
GARY: polos?
TRISTE: yes
GARY: trebors!!! Trebor mints are a little bit longer
DENVER & TRISTE:
            Yes I remember
TRISTE: at the bus stop by the chippie
GARY: and your little brother checking on us -
TRISTE: aye and when i mentioned foreplay you went and
            got your friends to...
GARY: i thought you meant...
TRISTE: yes Gary yes - it always seemed to either be totally
            pissing down or be so sunny you could walk
            barefoot on the pavement didn't it?
GARY: then
DENVER: then then then then........
TRISTE: do you remember the first time we
GARY: did it like
DENVER: but it was always there they they THEY were always
            there waiting waiting - to to... ah fuck the words
            choke my throat now even now now... to to bully
            to beat... that loneliness that playground loneliness
            of unbelonging of waiting all day for my mam to
            come and get me and take me home, home...
TRISTE: yes - did it -
GARY: yes i can still remember it - it was always warm and
            cosy
TRISTE: yes you didn't mind the heating being on then cos
            you didn't pay for it -

GARY: It was winter -

TRISTE: yes and i remember you begged me to dress with no knickers on

GARY: and you told me not to put any pants on - walking down stairs like John bastard Wayne i was - like sum huge fuckoff secret -

DENVER: secret secret - hide hide away... away...

TRISTE: you spent the first 10 minutes shagging the carpet!!!

GARY: well i di'n't know - it felt nice ...

TRISTE: still tight then weren't you though

GARY: how do you mean?

TRISTE: well used the johnny twice didn't you!!

GARY: just seemed a bit offa waste really

TRISTE: yeah after 10 seconds i s'pose it did!!!

GARY: i knew this bloke right he used to put one dunkey on over another cos he was paranoid about getting his girl pregnant

TRISTE: cor couldn't do that could you Gar - 2 johnnies - tha's your weeks supply gone eh!!!!

DENVER: intimidate   swagger

GARY: ok ok - jus' careful tha's all - sex is a funny thing innit?

TRISTE: was with you

GARY: Oh i i never realised

TRISTE: Sorry

DENVER: push around persecute - and the thing is they never knew they never knew they were doing anything wrong and to this day they never will acknowledge what they did - like a selected amnesia

GARY: so anyway - sex aye fucking funny thing innit - all tha' for five minutes of flapping about then off to sleep like - weird

TRISTE: yes well speak for yourself

DENVER: but i can't forget cannot forget - i have to have to commemorate - work through things have to - some say i got a chip on my shoulder some may say i am revenge - no: i only want to know why - to ask to elicit a dialogue - to know -

GARY: need a shag?

TRISTE: no -

TRISTE: Gary - wha's gone wrong say - why why are w-we so...

DENVER: torment *(looks at wrists)* torture

GARY: *(serious)* oh cum on mun love it's not that bad we're gonna have a baby in no time - then it'll be ok - won't it - look i

TRISTE: but bu-but i'm i'm in the middle of my course - its not the right time -

GARY: when is it the right time say mun love?

DENVER: coerce

TRISTE: i mean you're on leave from the army - we haven't got much money - how how we gonna afford a pram and all the stuff for the little one say Gary -

GARY: i know people... who.

TRISTE: when you going back to the army say?

GARY: *(awkward, guarded)* oh not yet want to be 'ome with the little one mun - Tris - wanna be there when he's born like - you always say i'm gone too much now I'm 'ome and you want me to go back again - fucks me up mun - i i i

TRISTE: I'm just worried about the money tha's all - i thought you get money if you're on leave anyway?

DENVER: to bulldoze to overbear to to

GARY: there's some delay - i phoned yesterday

TRISTE: Where from?

GARY: i used a phone box

DENVER: i just want to speak to to communicate to ask why why why?

TRISTE: Really!

GARY: i used a phone box

TRISTE: oh right...

Triste leaves

DENVER: bully - i am scared to say the word it cakes my arteries spits in my eyes layers my soul fucks my mind ...... bully bullied bullying *(shouts)* bully .... STOP!!!!!

GARY: see i i told them that i i had to - please lisssen to me - please - see my eyes see them - they have been there they have seen things that i wish made me blind - they have cried and raged hated and lost lost - please lissen to me - it gets so lonely - so lonely and everybody thinks you're mad just cos you speak your heart after you have been made to think yours has died died - please lissen - will you - will you - its n-not all bullets bruises fucks and fists hate and anger, anger - can you yer me can you is there anybody left on this earth tonight this viagra'd space this prozac wilderness this lithium clinic this loneliness so deep i can lick it - this place - please why do they call me dumb when it is they that are deaf - lissen lissen to the stars in dead skies, stars in dead skies skies ....

Bullets - machine guns - crowds - panic - industrial noise - very loud and shocking -

*GARY crashes down and hides under the table clutching it - the
            sounds subdue to be replaced by radio signals and
            marching and general army sounds -*
GARY has reverted back to childhood -

GARY: (*making gun noises*) - peeoow - do da dddddd
             yeoow - i killed you - bang bang - you're dead -
             ready or not coming - johnny where are
             you - johnny - i'm coming - johnny - yow ya yow ya
             yow - ne nah had you - come on let's play war -
             let's play war - can i be the goodies can i cani please
             -

DENVER: TEN!
GARY: quick hide hide hide -
DENVER: NINE!
GARY: get the bullets boys now -
DENVER: EIGHT!
GARY: now
DENVER: SEVEN!
GARY: oh look there's a rainbow -
DENVER: SIX!
GARY: look up up inna sky a rainbow -
DENVER: FIVE!
GARY: where does tha' come from 'en - say say -
DENVER: FOUR!
GARY: can i go in goals say - please can i - i'll be - neville
             southall right - ok - carn get a goal past me - for a
             toffee flea -
DENVER: THREE!
GARY: why can't i cry - say why -
DENVER: TWO!
GARY: i want to i want to - why can't i cry?

DENVER: ONE!
GARY: DAD DAD DAD!.........

EXPLOSION

DENVER: Right my son, boys DO   NOT   CRY
              And if I catch you crying I will beat you so fucking
              hard you will never - NEVER - shed a single salty
              fucking tear again - boys will always BE in control
              know what to do in an emergency   no dolls
              kisses   no cuddles NOTHING   CHILD can you
              BOY I said can you
              THOU SHALT NOT

BOMB

Flat interior - throughout the scene DENVER is visible in his flat - he is cutting articles and images out of newspapers of serial killers, violence, riots, male sexual perversion - male issues etc., etc. He sticks his fingers down his throat to be sick, then attempts to listen in to GARY and TRISTE's conversation as he looks through a hole in the ceiling down onto their flat -

TRISTE is sat watching TV doing her nails - it is about midnight on 30th December 1999 - a sudden burst of noise and the door swings open - GARY is standing there smiling clutching a half-empty bottle of wine - he is well built - he is obviously drunk - dressed in army fatigues

TRISTE: evening - where've you been then?
GARY: oh you are fucking posh aren't you tonight - out
           tha's where out - 'ow bout yew?
TRISTE: been yer waiting for you - watching tele - drinking

horlicks you know - *(pats her stomach)* looking after little joe - normal things that's all - doing my project ..... its really getting .... *(gives up)*

GARY: i been normal as well - downa town - having a fucking laugh with the boys fucking old Flob headbutted a copper tonight - fucking blood everywhere - great mun - yeah!! one nil one nil one nil -

TRISTE: was he alright?

GARY: who Flob - yeah fucking great mun - ran off gone like the fucking wind mun - the fat fuck

TRISTE: no - the policeman mun - was he alright -

GARY: don't know - wen offinna ambulance - s'pose so - who cares mun -

TRISTE: oh well - nice night then - see anybody out like -

GARY: yeah - hundreds - i mean its fucking christmas mun for fuck's sake - party time - fucking freebooze everycuntingwhere -

TRISTE: i wish you wouldn't say that word -

GARY: wha' - booze - booze booze boozing -

TRISTE: nah - the other one - the c word - it's just - it's just so - hard and cold like - like you -

GARY: you 'aven't got the heating on 'ave you - put a fuckin' blanket on mun - you know money an' stuff ...... and the lights fucking 5 lights on mun ....

TRISTE: no i 'aven't got the heating on - an' turn the lights off yourself -

GARY: oh fuck up mun - always on at me 'en you - carn please old fucking triste carn i - it's always can you do tha' can you say it like tha' mun - wha' am i your fucking puppet isit -

TRISTE: oh don't start now mun - it's late - i just said i don't like tha' word

GARY: oh right - well I I don't like your fucking words
           right -
TRISTE: like what?
GARY: like um er um like fucking shopping like fucking
           spending
           like sales like bastard beauty parlour and like
           cunting credit - there - tha's better - words fucking
           words -
TRISTE: - and your favourite words - oh we carn afford that
           mun doll - carn you get it cheaper mun - go on
           bugger off to bed - leave your clothes in a heap for
           me - break wind loudly as you snore and if I'm
           lucky i may get off with being able to get out of a
           dry bed in the morning - now there we are - words
           fucking words -
GARY: i'm just careful with money that's all
TRISTE: careful - tighter than a camel's arse in a sandstorm
           you mean
GARY: - you're sexy when you're angry you know tha' -
           turns me on - do you.....
TRISTE: oh think you're James Bond isit well you're not
           getting near me tonight - you may as well go an
           have a wank now if you want - in the bog - go on -
           i'll pass the tissues - and why do you still wear those
           clothes mun say?
GARY: fuck up right i do what i want - just makes me feel
           ..... do you know you really
TRISTE: oh dear yer we go - what - i look sexy when i m
           cleaning now isit - hey boy?
GARY: fuck up - i told you about the boy stuff right - hold
           on i'm speaking mun - since you did tha' soc - tha'
           socio - that fucking ology thing uppa nightclass
           youreally fucking changed aye - everycunting thing

- from shagging to cooking to cleaning - you you question everything - everything mun - why?

TRISTE: look we just think differently about certain things mun - i don't want to talk about it now mun - wha' will little joe think mun - don't you ever think about him - little one in there say?

GARY: yes, yes i do think about him in there right - ok - course i fucking do - it's just - i i ....

TRISTE: ok ok - look it's late - i'm tired you're drunk -

GARY: *(sarcastically)* i'm clever you're thick - i got a-levels you're unemployed - lalalala - fucking 'ell mun - this is just boring - as boring as all your fucking books .... why do you need all these then if YOU are so fucking clever then?

TRISTE: *(gets up to leave room)* they're for my course - help improve the mind - try it some time - I'm off to bed

GARY: no you're not i wanna talk to you -
(Blocks her way)

TRISTE: oh cos you wanna talk then - that's ok is it - get the flags out mun - GARY wants to talk - hiphiphooray - wow! grow up -

GARY: triste - how to put a man down eh? fuck up with your fucking comments right - did tha' in your fucking sociolo - that fucking class did you -

TRISTE: a man eh now that's an interesting one - ah let's see - what is my little Gary's definition of a man - say - come on - i can't wait for this -

GARY: ah bollocks you don't give a shit about me and what i think - fuck me since i came back you've hardly fucking touched me mun - a man needs to be bastard held as well mun -

TRISTE: yeah but he's gotta swear in front of it first - yeah and a woman needs to be felt - no sorry a woman

	needs to be fucking felt - tha's better -
GARY:	- fuck me i came in quite happy like and wham up it goes like a fucking volcano - i may as well go out mun -
TRISTE:	go then -
GARY:	i will then -
TRISTE:	go on then -
GARY:	i fucking will 'en - you watch -
TRISTE:	i am
GARY:	right -

GARY leaves and slams the door - TRISTE nonchalantly looks around and winks at the audience -

TRISTE: six seven eight nine and .....
GARY *and* TRISTE *together:*
            i need to go for a piss first

GARY goes to the toilet - TRISTE waits - Gary returns

TRISTE: the army really changed you Gary it really fucking did mun -
GARY: yeah it did change me - it made me realise how life is ready to die at any minute and that there is always always some twat ready to kill you ready to tell you you're wrong and they're right - it made me realise how pathetic we all are - right - it made me realise how fucking evil humanity is - and out there - out there - i knew i could die and nobody nobody would have known my name or cared about me - i knew - that and it made me shit my pants - it really did - so - go on study your nightclass - go on
TRISTE: why you having a go at me say? why? look Gary

you'll never understand - out there in barracks with
all the little shitty wives waiting for their hubbies to
come home to food on the table and a shag on tap -
that's all you saw all you needed coupla pints
downa club black your face and off - and me me sat
at home waiting for tomorrow to come - it meant
nothing to me Gary - nothing -

GARY: always fucking moaning - too much too little - then
          you ran back yer - fucking deserted me out there
          you did -

TRISTE: couldn't go on like that - i wanted more - i got a
          heart as well mun gary - a life -

GARY: yeah yeah yeah - think you know it all don't you?

TRISTE: what - i i i -

GARY: But you know nothing have you ever seen a baby's
          body at the side of the road - i have and do you
          know the thing that really made me cry - do you
          know -

TRISTE: no what?

GARY: it didn't have any shoes on - it didn't have any
          shoes on and its little feet were just there so little
          and gentle so so so delicate there - but it had no
          shoes on - i i i just wanted to hold her and bring
          her alive again -

TRISTE: a time to love a time to hate -

GARY: *(tears - angry)* what?

TRISTE: nothing - just words - tha's all -

GARY: give it a rest mun - watch out the world is goin to
          fucking end! fucking one thing
          afterabastardnothermun - whooah -

TRISTE: a time to live a time to die......

GARY: look we're all fucking lost all fucking scared all
          fucking united by the fact that we're gonna die and

one day one day we will and and and that until
you've seen a dead body you know nothing nothing
how we're all fucking evil - man or woman - we are
all bastard killers - all of us - and out there - you
knew the meaning of life - you did love - and that
was death - and you'd do anything - anything to
dodge it or stop others being killed -

TRISTE: Gary - you scared of god?

GARY: *(cocky)* god who - where's he live........hahaha - nah why?
you?

TRISTE: yes s'pose i am - don't know wha's out there - need
something to cling to -

GARY: why?

TRISTE: just do - can't be all killing and evil can it?

GARY: nah mun you been watching fucking songs of praise
or summat mun - all fucking godsquad
alloffafucking sudden -

TRISTE: our father - which......

GARY: fuck up

TRISTE: yeah yeah little old triste silly little girl isn't she? ok
- look i'm tired an little one's kicking - i i i i think
i'll go to bed now - what's in the little bag say - you
always got it with you.....say?

GARY: it's nothing - nothing - good luck that's all - yes -
ok love - ok - i'll be there now -

TRISTE: bloody soldiers and good luck....night - night - a
time to weep and a time to......

GARY: night -

*Sudden total chaos: air raid siren bombs dropping machine guns
then screams shouts panic planes flying overhead blue lights red
lights -*

Gary gets out a scan picture from his bag

GARY: *(he struggles with every word as he cannot articulate his feelings easily)* Hallo little joe - one day when you're older you'll understand perhaps cos i don't know if i'll be around one day - it's not going to be easy - i can't really speak very well but you got be strong little one strong out there in that fuck ...... sorry .... world out there you gotta be who you want to be not who they want you to be - five fingers growing - but i don't know how to tell you that hands make a fist smash jaws push buttons hold knives to kill a belief in life

DENVER: more boys commit suicide than girls - suicide is a comforting thought suicide think about the word it - su   i   cide cide - the desire to end one's life - the desire - why we all ask why why why are we all yer - see me you i them them i can yer them stabbing voices into my mind - still fucking yer them them - how can i forget say how can i forget - voices faces eyes fists fists shouts and screams there - no place to run no place to hide - so why am i yer say yer now fear fractures forget - fucks mind into hate hate hate - see don't wanna hate don't wanna despise - you me i myself cry why look look these mountains that still bleed - still bleed - long to touch long to hold

GARY: five fingers growing harming nothing hurting no one - how can i hold you little one?
you gotta watch out you gotta stand like an oak tree in the wind and rain stand and be strong -

whatever they chuck at you and they will you gotta
stand and take it and sometimes being a boy or man
you gotta keep quiet about it and just get on with it
cos nobody will listen - it's ok - it's ok to cry at
things but don't let the bastards - those who'll put
you down - don't let them see they've beaten you
ok - stand stand....... fuck it's hard speaking
sometimes - but don't worry don't worry - you are
the mountain snow melting the sunflower sleeping
the sad sun setting the lips speaking the heart my
heart breaking - i'm sorry i let you down i'm so
sorry i let you down - little one - see i i i can't tell
anyone this i i just can't - i - i - see I'll be your
Dad, your Dad forever ... for ... ever ....

Gary puts picture away and Denver turns lights on

*DENVER's flat - his flat is covered in photos, newspaper articles
about bullying, about serial killers, riots, anything male and
destructive - also - one wall is covered with lightbulbs so
when the light is switched on it is like a floodlight - very bright -
DENVER is talking to himself -*

DENVER: School   work   life .... yes sir - what could I
do about it - what - say what? WHAT? Voices in my
ears - posh boy swot fists in my side assembly - p.e.
showers alone   alone they said do it do it DO
IT!!!!!! I couldn't could I - I just couldn't could
never never make a fist - *(Tries to make a fist -
awkwardly)*
I WAS SCARED

GARY finishes and crawls over to the bed where TRISTE is sleeping peacefully - he starts to read from the Wizard of Oz - very slowly and painfully to her tummy -

GARY: and   the sc scare scarecrow wanted to go cos he didn't have a brain and he th tho thought the wizard would give him one .... then the lion jumped out and frightened them all - he said he only acted big and tough cos people expected him to - nice nice one ....

GARY tries to hold her -

GARY: triste - tri - please wake up - please - help me - i i i need you -

TRISTE: Gary - it's too late - please leave me alone - ok - watch it you're leaning on little joe - please now - go away -

GARY: i need you - triste please - i i i i - h h ho hol ho hold me please -

TRISTE: i know wha' your hold is - now fuck off gary please - now -

GARY: please please why do you just see me as evil please mun - hold me hold me - i i i

TRISTE: look don't get it all out of fucking proportion now isit - look just go to sleep - there's a good boy - shhshhh now - right - gary - we'll talk in the morning -

GARY: good little boy - what the fuck you mean - say - say

Getting agitated and angry - pushes TRISTE and tries to get on top of her -

GARY: hold me hold me -

TRISTE: leave me alone - leave me - all over the place -
           please

GARY: i said hold me - it is an order - IT IS AN ORDER!!!

TRISTE: what - what did you say?

GARY: an order - you must obey - obey - obey -
           (his eyes go wild and he stares at her - dangerous)

TRISTE: An order! - what you on mun gary - you're not in
           Germany now - stop - you're hurting little one -

GARY: he doesn't want to come out into all this anyway -
           poor sod -

TRISTE: right leave it now

GARY: i said it is an order - you gotta hold me - you gotta
           hold me -

TRISTE: please let me go - please mun -

GARY: can't can't gotta hold someone something i need to
           hold - to hold -

TRISTE: leave me alone - you're gone - fuck off - fuck off
           back to your war - go go g on

GARY: hold hold hold -

Denver between the noose and the door

DENVER: pathetic tosser you loser wanker quimmo bender
           fucker nothing - life fades everything breaks bastard
           useless dumb cunt - .... ah fuck - loser wanker
           nothing - hate myself - too thin too fat wimp clit
           mammy's boy fragile leave it all behind leave it all -
           it all - go go - it'll be better now - it'll be better - it
           won't hurt anymore - it'll slow it'll smile - i can be
           what i want - yes - they'll never know what they put
           me through - .... they will never know ....
           they will never know........... - oh mother of men

and mother of moths give me strength to enter the
heavy world again.............. this fucking world again
and again again and again.... - look at you - why
you doing this say why? - you loser - face it they
THEY beat you you little wanker toss pot go on
face up to it - they beat you - you believe them
don't you - .... oh mother of men and mother of
moths, moths .... in darkness
darkness must find the light ..... must find the
light......

HORSES

scene 2

MORNING - NEW YEARS EVE
slow awakening light as we hear groans and grunts - GARY is
lying on his back on the floor of the kitchen with a false pregnant
tummy on - he is saying - "breathe, push, breathe, one two three"
TRISTE enters almost laughs then remembers last night -

GARY: what?
(no answer)
GARY: sorry about last night - just a bit pissed tha's all
(no answer)
GARY: i said sorry - it was late -
(silence)
GARY: oh cum on mun love - please carn we jus' be
            normal for a while mun - please
TRISTE: and what is normal to you GARY say - getting blind
            drunk trying to rape me as if i was some object - say
            - you tell me wha's normal -
GARY: Sorry - hey gotta joke - want to hear it what ave

226

you dun wrong if your missus keeps coming out of
the kitchen to nag you - say - go on....

TRISTE: oh gary mun 'im not in the mood

GARY: you - you've made her chain too long...ha ha funny
innit......

TRISTE: yes very -

GARY: sorry - are we going out tonight - say?

TRISTE: dunno - fancy dress is it? *(laughs)*

GARY: *(shows off his tummy)* wha' - 'aven't you ever seen a
pregnant man before - don't know what allah
moaning is about - piece of piss!! but it's New
Year's Eve - - fresh start like -

TRISTE: yeah yeah

GARY: we haven't really had a good laugh for years 'ave we

TRISTE: .....wanna be interviewed?

GARY: what?

TRISTE: doesn't matter...............no we haven't - why?

GARY: jus saying tha's all -

TRISTE takes remote and goes to TV

GARY: you ok?

TRISTE: as if you care -

GARY: sorry -

TRISTE: why?

GARY: just am - sorry -

TRISTE puts TV on - News

GARY: you haven't put the heating on 'ave you - it's
boiling in yer mun

TRISTE: no .... GARY?

GARY: what now mun - g'on then put the ketttle on .....

	mind don't fill it up too much - just enough for two cups...
TRISTE:	i can't stand this anymore -
GARY:	ok put the fucking heating on - just put it on timer ... ok ... babe .....
TRISTE:	no
GARY:	stop fucking confusing me mun - look i was alright a minute ago
TRISTE:	were you - and little old me came in and caused all this eh?
GARY:	wha' - fucking PMT is it? here we fucking go ....
TRISTE:	other way round isn't it?
GARY:	tmp - tha's a new one -
TRISTE:	no stupid - i'm pregnant -
GARY:	i'm not stupid
TRISTE:	you're just like a little boy Gary you really are -
GARY:	fuck up i told you about that?
TRISTE:	about what?
GARY:	i'm not a boy ok - leave it right - now turn the fuck over right -
TRISTE:	no i wanna watch the news ok -
GARY:	i said turn it over -
TRISTE:	no
GARY:	you yerd - now turn it fucking over!

The news is on - we hear the main stories -

VOICE:	500 bodies have been found today inside the Kosovar/Albanian borders - most are unidentifiable - the little toddler who went missing on friday has been found in a black bin liner on a rubbish tip just outside .... the northern ireland peace process took a battering today as a nail bomb went off in

.... 60 people have been taken to hospital ....
statistics revealed today shows that suicide with
young men is the second biggest killer after road
accidents and that the most common age for male
suicides is 29 - posh spice's underwear reached a
record price at auction today - the lace knickers cost
a fan £2000 today .... and a report out today says
that today's men are the most confused they ever
have been.......that's the headlines on the last day of
the millenium - have a great night -

*GARY has become glued to the TV - in a world of his own as he
listens intently to the news. TRISTE turns the TV off - Gary still
stares*

TRISTE: Gary what's the matter - Gary
GARY: be quiet i'm lissening -
TRISTE: GARY!!!
GARY: i said be quiet - i'm lissening ok - ofuckingk!!
TRISTE: What!
GARY: go
TRISTE: what?
GARY: go going gone gone going - quick hide -
TRISTE: what you saying Gary - say gary - what you talking
            about? GARY - speak to me - please -
GARY: silence - quick hide - i smell fear - over there -
            number 4 - inside - down - hide i said hide - it is an
            ORDER!!!!
TRISTE: ok right - Gary - stop it please - please stop - stop!
            or i'm going to have to call the doctor -
GARY: blood we need a hospital - quick down - i said
            down - hide - it's over there - look bodies - bodies
            there - check if still breathing - well - are they -

TRISTE: Gary snap out of this - oh god please -

GARY: reload - fire - burn them out of number 12 - now -
           ok - they're vermin - i know - still - burn them out -
           this is war not fucking blue peter - now move ok
           ok!!!

GARY: WATCH OUT !!!! Friendly fire - fire!!

TRISTE leaves to go to DENVER's flat

DENVER: i just wanna run run up up into within into the
           mountains - just to see if they're still up there - still
           up there waiting for me - still still still...............the
           ponies - the ponies...........

TRISTE bangs on the door and opens it

TRISTE: Excuse me but have you got a phone? Please can i
           use it?

DENVER nods to the phone

GARY: paratrooper - no pain no gain - we we we gotta lie
           low for a bit - til darkness falls - ok lads - hide -

TRISTE: *(on phone)* Hallo can you help me please? I need a
           doctor

GARY: bombers overhead

TRISTE: It's for my husband, he's not well

GARY: private stop fucking about and listen -

TRISTE: - I don't understand whats happening to him - he's
           out of control and I'm frightened

GARY: it's an order - ok?

TRISTE: What ?

TRISTE: Powell. Gary Powell, Flat 1, 12 Rudbeck House

.... Postcode? ... Does it matter? Look i need help now please

GARY: Quick - gas - gas - masks on - quick - on - i said -

TRISTE: Yes i know it's New Year's Eve

GARY continues war speak under the following conversation

TRISTE: No, I can't take him to the hospital, I'm six months pregnant
No, no drugs .... no alchohol
He's in the army - on leave from Kosovo
I'm scared and I can't cope - can you send a doctor now .... My name ...... I don't believe this .....
What is YOUR name? Yes yes please be quick though - what? Oh yes the number - the number is

DENVER: 765............

TRISTE: 765...

GARY: 24567 B paratroopers Balkan division - quick i said watch out watch out its on fire - fucking hell you cunts move it move it - on on on it's too late - fuck white is hit - -

TRISTE: please hurry - please!!!

TRISTE puts the phone down -

TRISTE: Sorry!

TRISTE opens door and exits

DENVER: *(beautiful - savours every words - v. eloquent - in a trance - warm)* and i'd run up to the mountains where they couldn't get me and i'd just walk and run - an' one day i went up there and i noticed that the white one - the woman one was walking a bit slower and laying down more so i went up closer and could see that she ....was pregnant - she was gonna have a baby - and it was so so lovely - they were like some young courting couple - the man pony just there waiting and watching over the woman one and i'd go up and take them sugar and .... i would go up there and just forget all the everythingness in my life and just breathe - i remember thinking how beautiful it must be to belong somewhere with someone -

GARY puts TV on and TRISTE enters

TRISTE: Gary

GARY: quiet , I'm watching the TV - it's good isn't it

TRISTE: Gary I can't cope with this anymore. Gary!

Gary: Yes

TRISTE: Who are you?

GARY: fucking hell mun another bastard course is it? why?

TRISTE: say, what is it to be a man?

GARY: you're mad you are really fucking mad -

TRISTE: whooah!! fucking mad i am all over the place - wham bam thank you sam - smash crash - whooaah watch out for those tanks - !!!!

GARY: bastard!

TRISTE: i want to know see because since you came back my life has been so unhappy so unbearable so empty so so so painfilled - i just don't know what to do - it all seems such a mess -

GARY: oh it's just the baby mun making you like tha' - what 'ave i been doing wrong mun? hey wanna arm

232

wrestle - cum on -

TRISTE: NO THANKS! shall i list them - oh gary - it's just fucked tha's all - what is it to be a man - tell me - please? man man man man.......

GARY: maybe you're the fucking one that needs the 'elp like -

GARY turns TV off

TRISTE: what is it?

GARY: man?

TRISTE: yes

GARY: dunno - fucking hard work really -

TRISTE: tell me -

GARY: oh wha's this 20 bastard questions - just is tha's all -

TRISTE: man man man

GARY: it's like a train inna fucking tunnel ok!

TRISTE: wow - tha's poetic for a soldier

GARY: why .... for a soldier?

He goes to dumbbells

TRISTE: man

GARY: woman

TRISTE: together

GARY: forever

TRISTE: forever - NEVER

GARY: see suck out my emotion then piss on it - typical bastard typical

TRISTE: ok - why then? Gary i am begging you - this is our last chance - i have had so much shit thrown at me - we are breaking apart - i just want to understand - that's all - how has it all changed - say? how have

	YOU changed? stop doing that mun -
GARY:	helps me concentrate - if i make my body strong enough i could take on anything - anything -
TRISTE:	does it work?
GARY:	dunno - always on at me innit you're a fucking angel en'yew -
TRIST:	get a fucking grip mun - we're finished -
GARY:	how? why?
TRISTE:	we are ... we are -
GARY:	breaking?
TRISTE:	broken
GARY:	i i i i thought things were ok - i i oh fuck me mun - Triste - cum on - it's ok innit? the baby?
TRISTE:	what is it to be a Man? say - man man man
GARY:	alright alright - leave it mun fuck's sake -
TRISTE:	well?
GARY:	i've got feelings too in allah this right - fucking feelings....
TRISTE:	right we're getting somewhere now - feelings eh?
GARY:	feelings
TRISTE:	fucks
GARY:	fucked
TRISTE:	fuckers
GARY:	fucked up
TRISTE:	fractured
GARY:	fragile
TRISTE:	feelings?
(pause)	
GARY:	yes
TRISTE:	no
GARY:	yes
TRISTE:	no
GARY:	see who's got the fucking problem?

TRISTE: problem

GARY: yes

TRISTE: feelings

GARY: yes yes yes please yer me mun for fuck's sake - please -

TRISTE: go on

GARY: trying to - fuck me -

TRISTE: speak

GARY: listen

TRISTE: feelings -

GARY: yes!

TRISTE: ok

GARY: Triste this is NOT a fucking game it's like you're punishing me for something i have no idea what - if you got something to say then fucking say it -

TRISTE: oh yeah - well how come you never let me speak - merely contain me - imprison me i am your voice - just like over in Germany -

GARY: bollocks i don't

TRISTE: do

GARY: triste we should be holding hands telling the baby stories waiting for the fireworks inna sky - not this - now - why?

TRISTE: why did you become a soldier -

GARY: to save people

TRISTE: kill

GARY: save

TRISTE: kill - all wars are about killing

GARY: where would we be without armies and people who are prepared to go an' fight and help others - look don't get me angry now triste - please -

TRISTE: anger? tell me about it - go on.....go on......

GARY: frustration

TRISTE: punch hit lash slash smash destroy - very male
words -

GARY: only cos the world wants them - for its fucking
conscience - oh fuck up - wha's all this got to do
with us for fuck's sake?

TRISTE: everything

GARY: nothing

TRISTE: every....

GARY: look i joined the bastard army cos there was fuck all
to do roun' yer an i 'ad nuffin from school - look i
needed to belong sumwhere - do summat - i
thought i'd be able to help others like - tha's all -
you can fucking talk you used to love the uniform
used to turn you on like a fucking light mun - until
you read sum book and fucked off from Germany
left me there - say didn't you - started your course
then you'd get all fucking weird about it and stuff -
remember?

TRISTE: i became aware that's all -

GARY: and i didn't ?

TRISTE: yeah but it's only a job you fucking live it 28 hrs a
day - fucking blacked out faces at breakfast - tha's
all you ever wear is army clothes - even now when
you're at home - you just want me in the house
waiting at the window for you, the fuckin' hero to
come home - waiting, pregnant stuck in prison -
you made me have this baby - made me -

GARY: i i i didn't - i just wanted us to be family - tha's all -
oh please - please *(head in hands)* please - stop it
fuck's sake - stop -

TRISTE: angry?

GARY: you are

TRISTE: are you?

GARY: why - look what d'you wan me to do - drop my kegs and chop my knob off and fucking pickle it eh? say?

TRIST: Nice idea

GARY: ha! i carn help it - i am me...

TRISTE: me

GARY: you?

TRISTE: me

GARY: look we've 'ad our ups and downs but we're ok ain't we?

TRISTE: Gary -

GARY: what?

TRISTE: nothing i've

GARY: something?

TRISTE: every everything - i i

GARY: look i didn't have a choice to go to Kosovo fucking Ireland bastard Bosnia you carn blame it all on men man can you - fucking 'ell from time started there's been fucking wars and killings and everything mun - and i know men have mostly fucking done it - but there's no choice mun we're all fucked we're all conditioned we're all labelled mun - fuck i sound like a bastard course now don't i - but you got such a thing against me and manhood - why? woman is just as much to fucking blame ...... she's not all fucking innocent..... you want us to be a certain fucking way...

TRISTE: like what?

GARY: you do - you love it when i've gotta bit of stubble and grease on my hands or summat -

TRISTE: oh yes - that'll stop the world's problems won't it that'll really put an end to masculinity's power won't it - oh i am sorry -

GARY: you know what i mean - men do this women do
          that but men don't do this when woman say? fuck
          you love the tarzan thing don't you - you've created
          us jus' as much as me
TRIST: you're wrong.....
GARY: bollocks.....
TRISTE: Gary
GARY: what?
TRISTE: I'm leaving

SILENCE

TRISTE: it's over - baby or not - i am so tired of it all - so
          fucking tired i want out OK?

DENVER: and i went up one morning inna winter - it was
          beautiful - bright blue you could see forever -
          forever - and there was nothing up there it was like
          a silence had taken over the whole mountain - the
          two ponies weren't there - i couldn't find them
          anywhere - i went up there another day and another
          and another - but nothing - no sign - and then one
          day i could see the brown one - the man pony
          stood right on the edge of the mountain just
          looking out out across the valleys - and I went up
          close to him - I thought he was frozen - but he
          wasn't - I saw his eyes blink and he was stood there
          like an oak tree stood looking down the mountain -
          the I saw what he was looking at - down below was
          the white pony - her tummy slashed open - her
          white coat splashed with the blackest red you've
          ever seen -

SILENCE

TRISTE: Gary .... d'you yer me.......say?

GARY: why why but why? - i mean fucking 'ell mun why? Triste please - what the fuck?

TRISTE: no more - sorry

GARY: sorry?

TRISTE: no more punches in the ribs no more pissing in the wardrobe no more orders no more swearing no more goodbyes on rainy winter platforms no more don't waste my money save the petrol don't put the heating on no more small rissole and chips no more no more - a time to keep and a time to cast away, away ....

GARY: but i ....

TRISTE: no listen it's my turn to speak

GARY: what about our baby - say

TRISTE: my my my baby

GARY: what d'you mean MY.....

TRISTE: like i said mine mi mine.......

GARY: what about me?

TRISTE: what?

GARY: what about me?

TRISTE: always the fuckin' same - me mine my me my mine me me me - like a fucking spoilt little boy tha's all you are and ever will be gary is a little boy who wants everything your own way and for your mammy to watch out for you when you fall over - cos your Daddy ......

GARY: STOP!   please triste come yer - please?

TRISTE: *(Shouts)* fuck off!!! leave   me   alone!!

GARY: ok ok .... no it's not ok - what the fuck's going on - whose baby is it say - you've been fucking someone else haven't you - say say who is it say - i'll kill the cunt - Triste - whothefuckishe? say say?

TRISTE: always the answer eh - violence - sort out the whole world won't it - GROW UP!!! - i'll kill the cunt - big warrior - bash your chest - stroke your cock - shoot the spunk - crack the neck split the head drink the blood - grow up will you - it's over end of fucking story - kill me if there anyone to kill - go on go on - you are a fucking orchid -

GARY: What?

TRISTE: beautiful but a fucking parasite - you'll kill everything jus' to get what you need - need -

GARY: shut up shut up - or i'll cut ....

TRISTE: what!

GARY: nothing - i i

TRISTE: go on go on big man man man me tarzan you jane go on go on!!!!!

DENVER: and there inside her was the little foal curled up tight like a frozen stone age man as if ...... as if .... it were sleeping - sleeping -

GARY: shut up shut up

TRISTE: i've just begun my love just begun -

GARY: shut up shut up -

TRISTE: nah - no more do this do that - shut this hold that i wouldn't i would will you don't you....fucking hell and all the time i thought i was the fucking mad one - but it's you you you -

GARY: shut up shut up or i will....... i i i ....

TRISTE: will what?

GARY: *(gets knife)* i will - cut you open like a fucking pig -

now shuthefuckup -

TRISTE: you don't frighten me

GARY: don't i

TRISTE: wage war on your world gary wage war on yourself for a fucking change!!!!!! go on go on -

GARY: *(cuts himself)* i i i haven't got a war anymore - i i i haven't got a war -

TRISTE: that's it i can't take anymore ok - i i i'm going to get my stuff and go ok go - i i can't take it any more - ok - it's gone gone gone - leave you to your sweet war gary - there's no more for life in it for me - go on go on - kill kill kill! i'm going ok - i'll get my stuff and go.....

GARY: you'll never leave me -

TRISTE: watch me -

GARY: you never will -

GARY goes up close to her and punches her in the tummy - she falls down clutching her tummy - he suddenly realises what he's done -

GARY: oh god - i i i'm sorry - i'm sorry - i i - please - please don't go -

wh wh where you're gonna go? to him isit?

silence

GARY: please - please i i i don't know what i'll do without you - please - please?

TRISTE manages to stand up - looks him in the eyes - GARY looks away

TRISTE: you would never have dared to do that when we were first together - you said i had the beautifulest body you ever seen - said you'd protect me from everything - everything Gary - now look at you - that is the last time -

GARY: why didn't you let me then?

TRISTE: too late for words - too many scars, scars...........

GARY: i'll fix things Tri - i i will - please let me - please - i i didn't mean to -

TRISTE: i'll get my stuff....

GARY: please don't go.....

TRISTE: i've gone.....

GARY: please don't -

DENVER: and the man pony stood there for weeks just watching over them - for weeks - then one day i went up and he'd gone gone - into the emptiness of the mountains - gone - and i never saw him again -

GARY: i said don't go - that is.....

TRISTE: an order?

GARY: don't go -

TRISTE: i've gone

DENVER: and then - i found out that a group of kids - kids - from my school had gone up and killed the pony - slashed it open with a bread knife and pushed it over the edge - gone gone gone - and i i always felt guilty for not doing anything about it - just let it happen though - but i i know who did it - i know - i know -

GARY: see little one live free live free live wild and free in the fields and trees and skies roam smile watch the stars talk to spiders and birds .... it's not fair - it's

not - too much too much hurt and pain - too much
cos they want you to taunt or be taunted bully or
be bullied, hit or be hit, frighten or be frightened -
see it's just like in the book just like in the Wizard
of Oz - the lion only acted ard cos they wanted him
to - i i i was lost - i am i am lost - lost - did things
that still twist my stomach now but i can't speak of
it to anyone anyone on this whole sunlit earth - all i
hear is silence the silence of winter nights and valley
twilights where man meets man with fists and drink
- go your own way little one go - go........ five
fingers growing of man with without the blood
bleeding bled hold hold hold on.............see little
one - i had i had to run away run away from it all - i
i i couldn't take it anymore - see - over there in the
army - they would beat you hurt you push you into
a corner - too much too much - and no one no one
would lissen to me - i was so frightened little one so
so frightened and i i i couldnt talk to anyone - ok -
it's me an you against the world - ok - ok - my
lickle star, star ... see Ill be your Dad, Dad for ever
and ever my little star star ...

*GARY is sat with the candle's flame again - he ritualistically gets
dressed in his army gear and puts camoflaugue stick on - it is like
he has become another person - almost schizophrenic -
He lights the candle*

GARY: 10, 9, 8, 7, 6, 5, 4, 3, 2, ONE *(Blows candle out)*
EXPLOSION

TRISTE knocks on DENVER'S door - DENVER answers it -

TRISTE: *(out of breath, nervous, looking over her shoulder)* i'm
          sorry - can i come in a minute?

DENVER: yeah - course - what's the matter? Do you need the
          phone ?

TRISTE: no - can i just come in please -

DENVER: yeah come in - you look like you've seen a ghost -

TRISTE: Look i just need....

DENVER: how long you got?

TRISTE: sorry

DENVER: you know - how long till the baby? -

TRISTE: oh yeah - it'sa while yet - bloody warm in yer innit -

DENVER: yeah gotta be warm - babies like it warm in yer innit
          -

TRISTE: yes - yes -

DENVER: boy or girl?

TRISTE: dunno - like a surprise but my husband is convinced
          it's gonna be a boy - look - carn we talk about
          something else - i -

DENVER: first one -

TRISTE: yes - first one - what do you do then?

DENVER: can i touch?

TRISTE: what?

DENVER: can i touch it - your tummy like - looks so lovely -
          so -

TRISTE: no - i i i um

DENVER: *(whispers)* i'll protect you - you're safe yer -

TRISTE: sorry

DENVER: do you wanna lie down - have a rest like -

TRISTE: no no it's ok - i'll

GARY starts banging on doors

GARY: Is anyone in there - i am armed and dangerous -
          please be warned - hello anybody in there - avon

calling - hello -

TRISTE: pplease don't tell him i'm here - please

DENVER: it's ok - i'll protect you now - it's safe -

GARY enters

GARY: wow it's fucking dark in yer - *(turns the lights on)* fuck me - it's like Cardiff fucking city - fuck me i'm blind i am i'm fucking blinded mun - Triste? Triste?

DENVER: alright

GARY: What the fu....whoareyouaen?

DENVER: welcome .... welcome to my world - what's the matter -

GARY: uh ah nuffin just a bit bright like -

DENVER: only lights

GARY: Triste? Triste you inyer say? Oh how many feminists does it take to change a lightbulb - say?

DENVER: Don't know

GARY: 5 - 4 to make committee and 1 to go and get her fucking boyfriend to do it - haha - good innit - that'll have 'em -

DENVER: see all lights - they help me see everything - everything that goes on - nothing is hidden - it's all there -

GARY: oh yeah - bright inney?

DENVER: shall i turn them off - say -

GARY: uh no - tha's ok - what d'you do 'en? I've never seen you around - shift worker are you -

DENVER: yeah yeah sort of - what do you want Gary?

GARY: how d'you know my name -

DENVER: you told me

GARY: i didn't

DENVER: you did - just now

GARY: when -

DENVER: just now -

GARY: i didn't

DENVER: oh yes you did

GARY: Oh no .... fuck me it's a fucking pantomime - shut up -

DENVER: - thin walls - sorry - i....

GARY: oh aye and what else can you fucking yer up yer - what are you anyway - who are you?

DENVER: DENVER......Denver Jones

GARY: wha' - tha' a nickname isit - i knew this bloke inna school whose nickname was shitarse - straight up now - there's one to introduce to yer parents innit - hiya mam - here's my new boyfriend - hello - hello shitarse

DENVER: no - it's my real name - DENVER - Why'd they call you Gary?

GARY: pretty normal innit - anyway -

GARY looks around the flat - he sees all the cuttings and words on the walls -

GARY: whasallthisen -

DENVER: what?

GARY: all this - fucking pictures mun - fuckin'ell - why do you do this - fucking kinky or sumthing say?

DENVER: oh it's nothing - nothing - it's just something i do - do you want a cup of tea?

GARY: may as well - got fuck all else to do

DENVER goes to make some tea -

DENVER: so - th the kettle's broke - i i.....

GARY: it's OK - only like it in a tinfuckinmug anyway -

*GARY babbles to fill the silence - DENVER squints his eyes,
looks at him as if he's inspecting him*

GARY: oh well -

Silence

GARY: see - she blames it allonnafuckingarmy - she doesn't
realise what men gotta go through like - since she
done tha' fuckin' course she fucking thinks all men
are fucking rapists nutters little boys she says little
fucking boys - a little boy doesn't know what it's
like to wake at 3am to go on fucking patrol inna
pissing rain and find fucking dead kids in a burnt
out house with their mam crucified do they -

DENVER: no -

GARY: she laughs when i say i like fighting - see - i don't
like punching some cunt out - i like being hit - i like
the cut the blood in my mouth the lump on my
head the black eye the ache inna morning - makes
me feel alive makes me feel i connected - that I AM
REAL - see - go on - hit me - go on -

DENVER: i don't like to hit - i

GARY: wha! see you don't get it and you're a fucking bloke
as well .... i think .... see a fucking trip to B and
Q or a cappucino's not gonna sort out my fucking
head right - go on fucking hit me - go on - it don't
matter -

DENVER: i said i don't like hitting......it...

GARY: it'll make me feel alive for a while - it'll make me
feel as if i connected with someone on this fucking
earth - come on - see years ago men 'ad summat to

do with their lives - something to rage against -
now we all sit down and watch fucking changing
rooms and fucking jerrybastardspringer - mind you
that piece is smart - fucking carol vord - you know
the one with the teeth - fucking carol smiley - sorry
- yes thasssaone - i'd dip my brush in her pot
anyfuckingtimemun - i'd put a fucking smile
onerface i'll tell you - go on hit me inna stomach -
go on butt - it's ok -

DENVER: no no no i told you i

GARY: do it i said do it

DENVER: i said i don't like hitting -

GARY: go on it's an order

GARY: i fucking love Triste mun - i really fucking do .....
we're gonna have a baby we are ...... a baby .....
yeah .... go on hit me - hit me mun - it's ok

DENVER: no

GARY: do it - ok - hit me -

DENVER: i told you - i don't like hitting - it reminds me.....

GARY: it is an order

DENVER: i said -

GARY: do it - wha' - chicken?

DENVER: bastard!!

DENVER hits GARY hard in the stomach
TRISTE walks out of the bedroom - GARY sees her - doesn't
quite register -

DENVER: i i i'm sorry

TRISTE: Gary - you ok - *(to DENVER)* what's the matter
with you - you've hurt him

GARY: i'm ok - i'm ok -

DENVER: he he's going to hurt you YOU - white pony brown

pony - kids - knives - white pony - baby - baby - bleeding bleeding ok - you're not going to stop me - she's mine - you you you won't hurt her again -

GARY: Triste - whatthefuck you doing yer say? Is....

TRISTE: nothing nothing i just came yer - i was frightened - that's all -

DENVER: i looked after her -

GARY: what!

DENVER: you yerd - i looked after her

TRISTE: look i i think we better be going - come on -

DENVER: you you can't go now - no - you can't - you're safe yer - safe -

GARY: Triste - is this the bloke say?

TRISTE: no - Gary -

GARY: Denver you been fucking my wife -

DENVER: i i i would never harm her -

GARY: fuck me - got a right one yer - look -

DENVER: no - you look - - you hit her she's pregnant - she....

GARY: yes - twat - i put it there -

TRISTE: i better go

DENVER: no - no

GARY: listen butt - i don't know what or who you are -

DENVER: don't you - should -

GARY: why - been on crimefuckinstoppers have you? Ladies and gentlemen watch out for the nutter in flat 2 -

DENVER: forever the same - forever -

GARY: do you know who i am - i could slit you open

TRISTE: Stop it now Gary - let's go........

DENVER: yes - i know you very well - Gary Gary Powell still the same - forever the.....

GARY: cut the riddles wanker - outta way -

DENVER: go on hit me in the stomach - go on go on -

TRISTE: stop it stop it -

DENVER: sorry - sorry -

GARY: well then - this is fucking cosy innit - so
            "Mr.Weirdo" how come you and me are sat yer on
            New Year's Eve 199fuckin9 with my wife telling me
            she's leaving me and suddenly i know you and you
            know me say - what the fuck is tha' all about say?

DENVER: i've known you all my life - all of my fucking life

GARY: dunno what you mean butt -

TRISTE: i know - what if i leave and you two can sort things
            out eh -

DENVER: no you're safe yer - please

GARY: Triste - you stay right where you fucking are -

TRISTE: what?

GARY: you yerd - button it - i need to talk to you pair -
            wha's goin on?

DENVER: don't speak to her like that

TRISTE: i have to go - i i

DENVER: no it's ok - i'll protect you

GARY: what's it to you - fuckin' weirdo -

DENVER: she's she's -

GARY: i know i know we'll have a little competition is it -

TRISTE: grow up - Gary - in case you have forgotten - i am
            leaving ok - leaving - can you spell tha' - le a v
            ing - going going GONE ok?

GARY: what did you say?

DENVER: leave her -

TRISTE: it's always some sort of a competition - life's one
            big game isn't it Gary? And you - you always gotta
            come out on top - he-man Gary always gotta come
            out on top - and look at you - you can't even write
            a note for the milkman without asking me how to
            spell pints - ha - big man -

GARY: what the.........

DENVER: leave us alone - leave us -

TRISTE: no no no - you listen to me - you cannot go on like this - always the one in control always the one in charge always the one making others feel nothing - no no no - take a look at yourself Gary -

GARY: you bastard you fucking cunning cunting fucking bastard eh! Fucking hell - after all these years all this life you turn around and say that - god - and you've been thinking that all fucking along - is it any wonder I scream and shout is it any wonder i go downa pub is it - isfuckingit -

TRISTE: your words don't frighten me

GARY: fuck off - right yer we are DENV - *(Goes to candle)* there we are - see how long you can keep it in - ok - prove yourself - go no go on

TRISTE: Gary -

GARY: leave it woman - this is men's stuff - take a good fucking look - right - this is between me and my new friend - go on

DENVER: no

GARY: go on watch me - *(Hand in candle)* there tha's better - pain - good for the soul - soul - 5...4...3...2...1 yes! There you are butt - beat that 'en?

DENVER: no - i said -

GARY: do it do it do it

DENVER blows out candle

DENVER: I'll protect you now it's ok it's ok

TRISTE: it's time i left - it's over - over.....

DENVER: no no - it's ok - we're together now - now

TRISTE: I'm...

DENVER: i've been looking after you i've been watching you
            listening to you night after night day after day - I'd
            run up and see you and the tummy would be
            getting bigger and bigger and you walk slowly over
            to meet me and i'd give you bread and sugar - and
            the sky would blaze blue and you'd run off - so
            lovely so so so pure -

TRISTE: i...i...

DENVER: but now you're here - it's ok - it's ok - you're here
            and it's warm and i i can be the brown pony - i can
            look after you i....i...

GARY: what the fuck is going on -

TRISTE: i .... i ..... i ... i'm Triste - i'm not pregnant - i i i i -
            oh god -

DENVER: no you are

GARY: Triste - Triste - wha' - wha' you talking about -
            Triste -

DENVER: you are you are - my pony - my mountain -

GARY: what about this - *(Shows the scan)* it's all tha's kept
            me going - it's...whosefucking baby is it say? SAY?
            SAY!

TRISTE: - no more hurting - no more - it is your baby it is
            our baby ... it was our baby

GARY: what d'you mean Triste ... Triste .... our .... our
            baby ... our .....

TRISTE: dead ... our baby died Gary ... gone

GARY: how ... Triste ... wh wh why didn't you .....

TRISTE: couldn't speak .... frightened .... felt i'd failed ...

GARY: he's beautiful ...... so beautiful

TRISTE: you killed it..........

GARY: what did you say?

TRISTE: i said you killed our baby - i lost it after you pushed

	me down the stairs - you .... that's why i came back here -
GARY:	no no - you fell - i didn't push you - Triste - please - our baby - our baby
TRISTE:	gone - a time .....
GARY:	...... that's why i came home just to be with you .... you and the little one .... i ran away .... they're after me .... just to be home yer with you and .... no no .... please - help me HELP ME
TRISTE:	No Gary - no - all these months i've kept it inside - held my tongue smiled when i've wanted to cry - all this time i've played along - pretending - whispering in the dark - asking God for an answer - afraid to upset you - you YOU! - praying it all didn't happen and that that photo would grow and grow and ...... it would be alright -
GARY:	Please
TRISTE:	No Gary - no more - i can't go on
GARY:	Get away from her -
DENVER:	y y you can't do this - y you you've done it again - bastard! I'm i'm protecting her -
GARY:	Fuck up - get away - see this - this is my protection
DENVER:	you killed my baby my my pony - you killed it see see the blood the blood running - it's always there always - gone - you bastard - you - you -
GARY:	i i didn't ....
DENVER:	- you've spoilt it all - j just like before -
GARY:	dunno what you're on -
DENVER:	you do - come on Gary - you remember - must have told all your friends from school about it - yer - remember - up yer - beneath this sky - can't you smell it can't you - remember - you came up yer - you killed her - you killed my pony - yyou slashed

her open - remember - up yer on my mountain -

GARY: shut up shut up

DENVER: she was pregnant - she had a little baby inside her -

GARY: shut up shut up

DENVER: just like now - eh Gary - just like now - now leave us -

TRISTE: please stop it - stop it both you - there is nothing nothing here nothing

TRISTE leaves - removing bump

GARY: fuck up - i ......don't know what you're......

DENVER: oh you do Gary - i'm sure you do - look at my eyes - it's me ...... Denver - Denver Jones - from school - see - remember - remember kicking the shit out of "SHITARSE" remember making me eat dogshit remember cutting my hair ripping tipping ink into my mouth remember those names names

GARY: stop it i i ...

DENVER: wanker tosser quim twat poof ponce cripple cunt runt mammy's boy mammy's boy .... listen to it listen to it ....

GARY: stop it stop it - fuck up or i'll ....

DENVER: listen ...... listen

GARY: i i i am .... i .... i am ....

DENVER: understand now - now leave us - go go we are free - it's safe - now leave - leave - you are not wanted yer on my mountain with my pony under this beautiful sky - you do not belong - now fuck off!!!!!!

TRISTE enters without pregnancy

TRISTE: it's over Gary - it's over - no more lies no more

illusions - a time to laugh and a time to cry.....to
cry........a time to live and a time to die......to die -

Huge pause

TRISTE: Gary?
TRISTE: Gary?
GARY: yes
TRISTE: where you been?
GARY: i i don't understand -
TRISTE: i said where have you been for the last 5 years of our fucking marriage say? downa pub downa gym out witha boys arseholed ratarsed fucked up .... dead dead dead .... say Gary - where have you been -
GARY: i'm sorry - i'm ......i don't know.........i i i don't know what to do any more i i don't know .... where to fit in ...... i'm sorry
TRISTE: sorry - sorry - is that all you can say - SAY? Isit - fucking sorry - you're a killer GARY - a fucking murderer - you're a man Gary and you never knew the pain you caused cos you've never never felt any yourself - ok - a fucking murderer .... take your clothes off - now
GARY: i -
TRISTE: now i said take them off - it is an order .... a fucking order i tell you take them off ....
GARY: ok o k o k *(Takes his army clothes off)*
TRISTE: there - how does it feel say .... what you're gonna do now? ...... pardon i didn't quite yer that Gary - you're nothing Gary - fucking nothing .... all you care about is you - you and your little world - Gary Powell -

GARY: please - please - .... i'm sorry -

TRISTE: sorry sorry sorry - shut up shut up - you don't even
             know the meaning of the word - fuck off - what
             about my baby what about my life my heart my
             fucking soul say - Say! Look at you - you're a
             fucking killer - KILLER!! .... a time to live and a
             time to die ......

TRISTE moves towards GARY with the knife

DENVER: no more fighting no more blood - no more no
             more ....

TRISTE: *(Throwing knife away)* fuck it this won't help save
             me from all the pain you've inflicted - ever! Fuck it
             - Gary, you will never hurt me again -

TRISTE starts to rip up scan

TRISTE: i'm sorry little one - so so sorry - you are a star now
             - shining shining .... up up in the dead skies,
             dead skies ....

GARY: please don't Triste - i ....

TRISTE: a time to stay and a time to leave..........to leave -

TRISTE exits

GARY: murderer? I don't know ...... what ...... to ...... say -
             sorry - sorry -

DENVER: say nothing .... feel everything ....

GARY: why did you stop her?

DENVER: what

GARY: stop her killing me - say - would have been for the
             best - i've fucked things up so much -

DENVER: i've seen too much blood too much dying - i i can't stand it any more - i cannot cry anymore - my eyes have been bled raw from seeing - i cannot cry anymore - i am dry .... dry .... emptied out ......

GARY: see - when i was a kid my mam told me that my dad had died and .... well - that he'd gone up to heaven like - so i wandered round for months looking up to the sky hoping to see him up there with the stars or when it was sunny - but i never saw nothing - but then one day mam was late picking me up from school and i was waiting by the gate in the pissing rain and i saw my dad on the other side of the road - he wasn't dead - no - so i stood there thinking he must have come down from heaven like - uh fuck .... bastard!!!!! he was pushing a pram .... he didn't see me .... i ..... he just walked past .... it .... i never told no one about it not even mam like - and that night i went home and went to bed and stuck sellotape over my eyes to stop me from crying and i just wanted to be able to be a dad to this - tha's all - tha's all - to never walk past his schoolgates and not see him .... never .... NEVER! NEVER!! whatever i've done to this this fucking world .... this fucking world has done to me .... no more fighting no more bullets ... i'm sorry - wage war on ourselves -

DENVER: no more pain ....

GARY: no more pain forever and ev - it's cold in yer innit

DENVER: cold up yer on the mountain - can you see the stars up there can you feel the dew ....

GARY: yeah ..... yeah .... the mountain .... yeah ....

DENVER: forever and ever

TRISTE: sing to me sweet mothermalesing to me across the
            swollen wounds of our lives sing sing to me -
            whisper words of comfort not this violence verse -
            sing to me unity not division sing to me of love not
            hate - mothermale learn unlearn sing to me of soul
            stay yourself but push yourself further further to the
            tomorrow - sing to me of closing closeness sing to
            me of tears tearing at your throat sing to me of
            tenderness —— sing to me -

the end